THE LITTLE GIANT BOOK OF

OPTICAL ILLUSIONS

Keith Kay

Sterling Publishing Co., Inc.
New York

Library of Congress Cataloging-in-Publication Data

Kay, Keith.
The little giant book of optical illusions / by Keith Kay.
p. cm.
Includes index.
ISBN 0-8069-6174-0
1. Optical illusions–Juvenile literature. I. Title.
QP495.K38 1997
152.14'8–DC21 97-417

30 29 28 27 26 25 24 23

Published by Sterling Publishing Co., Inc.
387 Park Avenue South, New York, N.Y. 10016
Excerpted from *Take A Closer Look: The Big Book of Optical Illusions & Visual Oddities* first published in Great Britain by Bright Intervals (Brinbo) Books

Distributed in Canada by Sterling Publishing
℅ Canadian Manda Group, 165 Dufferin Street,
Toronto, Ontario, Canada M6K 3H6
Distributed in the United Kingdom by GMC Distribution Services,
Castle Place, 166 High Street, Lewes, East Sussex, England BN7 1XU
Distributed in Australia by Capricorn Link (Australia) Pty Ltd.
P.O. Box 704, Windsor, NSW 2756, Australia
Printed in China

Sterling ISBN-13: 978-0-8069-6174-3
ISBN-10: 0-8069-6174-0

Welcome to the Magical World of Optical Illusions. This is a book that will put you to the test to see if you can "believe your own eyes"!

What is an optical illusion? Basically it's something you see that is not exactly what it appears to be. Some of the pictures at first glance seem "normal," but look again and you will see some surprising things!

There are many types of visual illusions, and I have tried to make this book varied and interesting with many examples from around the world. Many of them are new, but some are very old.

I enjoyed compiling the material, and hope that you will find this a book to enjoy, to dip into, and to be fascinated with. Above all, have fun and . . .

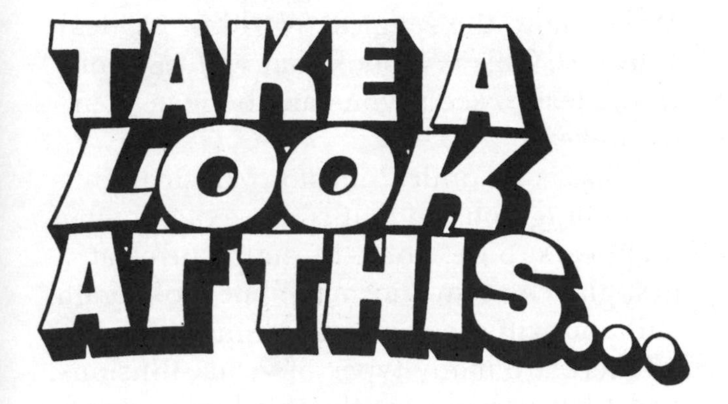

Answers are in the back of the book.

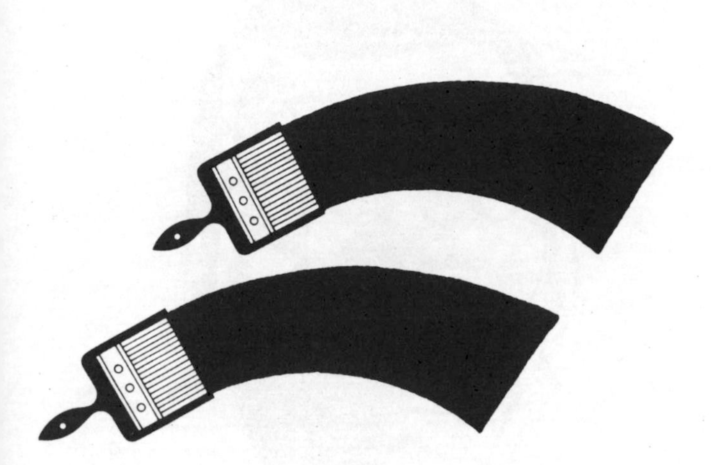

Which one of these two painted stripes is longer?

W.H. Hill is signing the visitor's book. This signature first appeared in *The Strand Magazine* in 1908. Why is it odd?

Very slowly read the words in the hat.
What do they say?

What do you see in the middle of the frame? Is it a letter “B” or the number “13”?

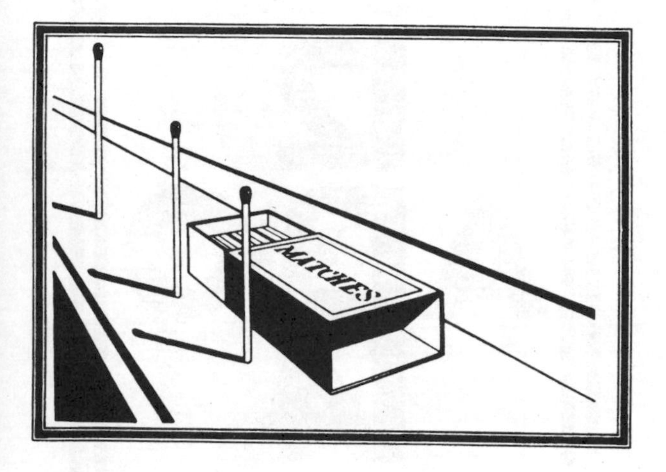

Which match is biggest?

Rotate the page in a circular motion. What happens?

Stare at this skull for about 30 seconds (try not to blink) – and then look at a sheet of white paper. What do you see?

What is mysterious about these donkeys?

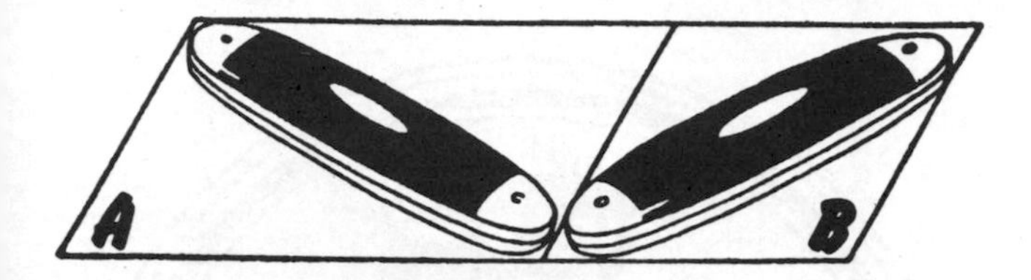

1. Which of these two knives is bigger? Take a guess.

2. How do you pronounce the word above? Think about it.

The chef is holding a cake – but one piece is missing. Where is it?

This old drawing is a satirical print of a monkey. Who do you see if you turn the print upside down?

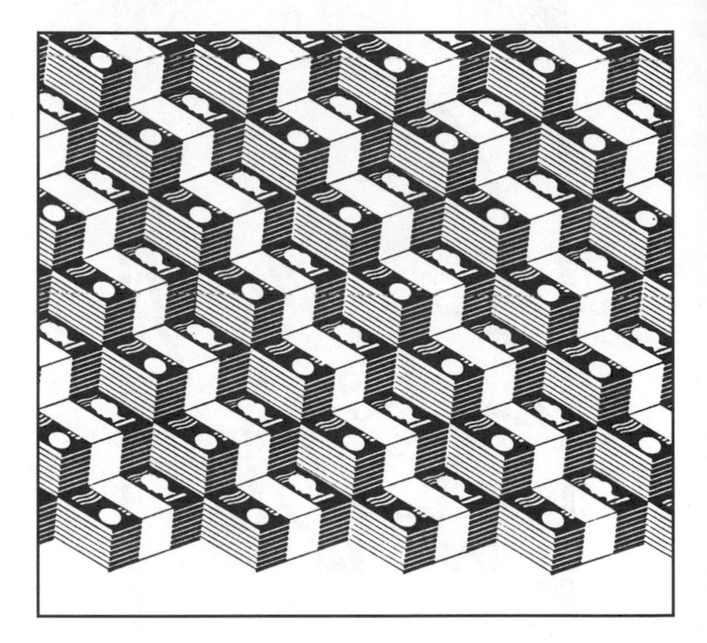

Are these stacks of banknotes sloping downwards to the right, or are they pointing down to the left?

At first glance, we see a pig. But where is the farmer?

What are you looking at – the inside of a tunnel – or the top of a mountain?

Stare at the center of the illustration. Then slowly bring the page close to your face. What happens?

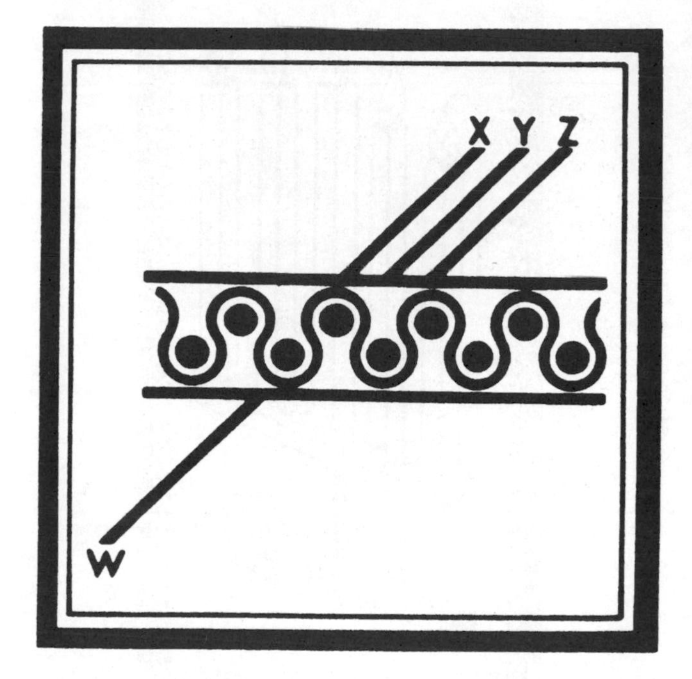

Which line connects with the letter "W"?

How many candles are there?

The famous magician Dunninger used this design as a logo. Do you notice something odd about his features?

This jockey is sad. Can you find his happy employer?

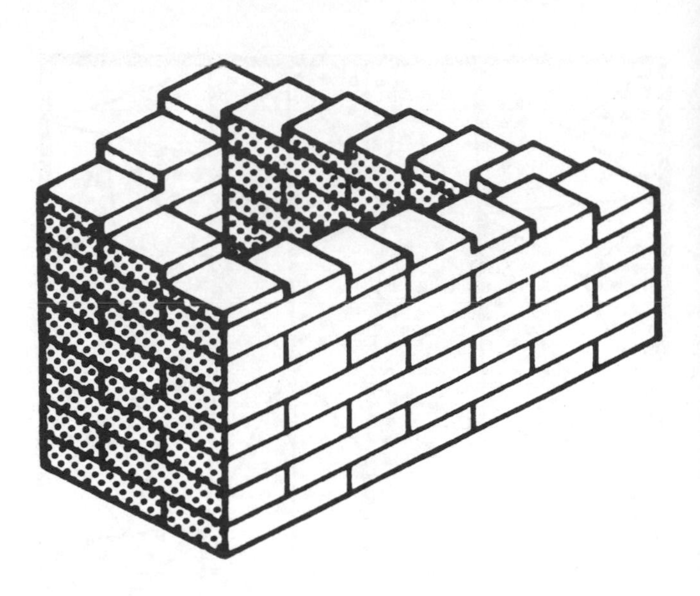

Point to the top step. Now point to the bottom step. What's the matter?

Can you find the five-pointed star hidden in this mosaic?

a. Do you recognize this old proverb? Is it correct, as it is written here?

ROTATOR

b. What is unusual about this word?

The four portraits on page 29 were published over a hundred years ago. If you view the page as in the small sketch above, you will see them in a better perspective. They are, left to right, the Princess and Prince of Wales, Queen Victoria – and who is that fellow on the right?

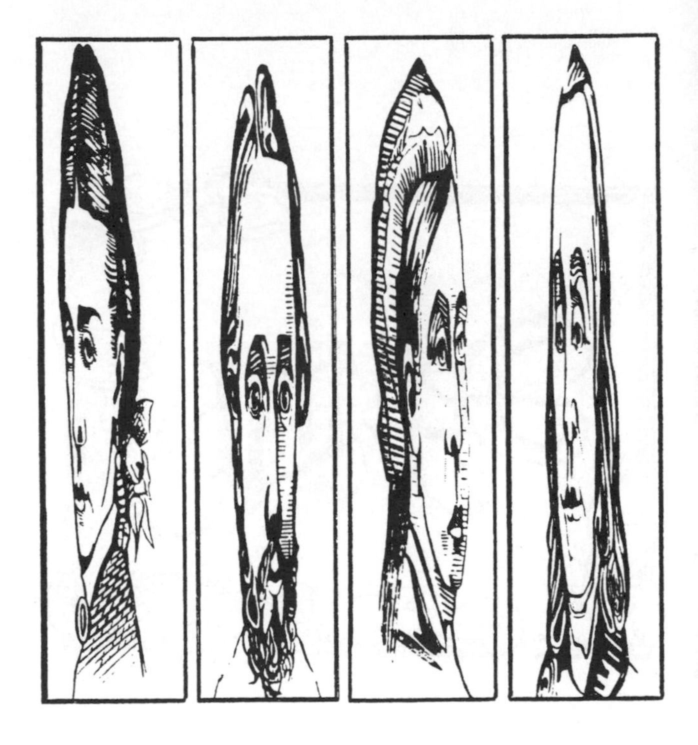

Is there life after death?

Is the zebra white with black stripes or black with white stripes?

Does this drawing show four white arrows – or a black letter "H" in a white diamond?

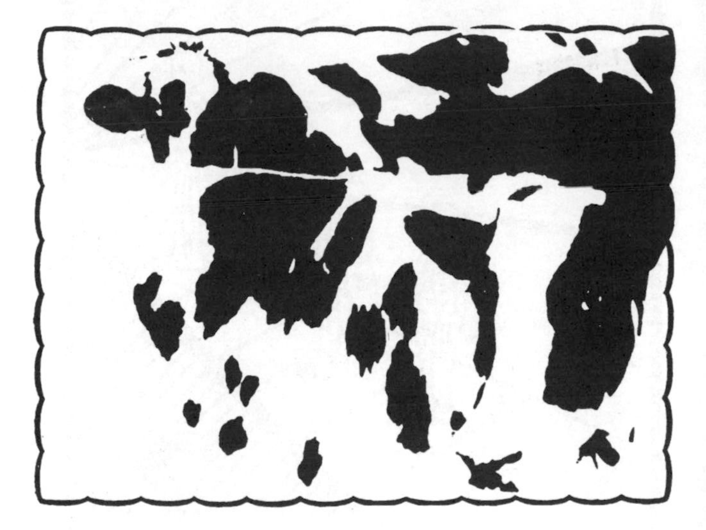

Can you find the black and white cows?

Which skeleton is the biggest?

Look at the intersections of the white lines. What do you see?

Can you spot the 15 differences between "A" and "B"?

B

Turn the year 1881 upside down and it looks the same. Turn the page around and see. When was the previous topsy-turvy year before 1881?

a What number has been hidden in the letters of this word?

b Which distance looks bigger? Is it a-b? Or b-c?

This is Garibaldi. Turn him upside down and who does he become?

What do you see – black wine glasses or white vases?

Which thin line looks bigger – A or B?

The old wizard can change himself into animals. What animal is he changing himself into now?

Would you describe the back wheel of this cycle as a circle?

The round shapes in the jar are strange. Look at them from a distance or squint your eyes and what happens?

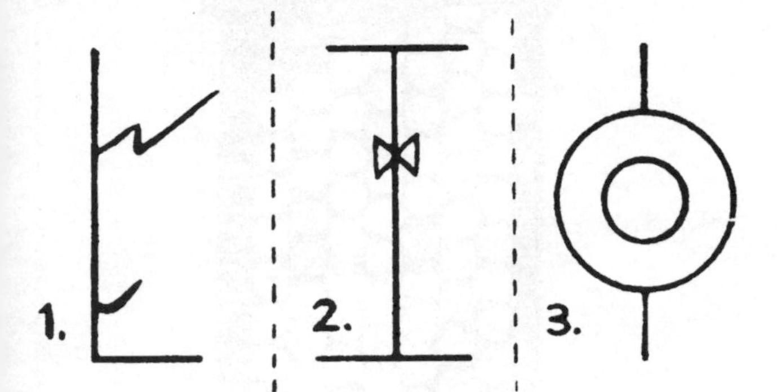

Here are 3 puzzle drawings. Can you figure them out?

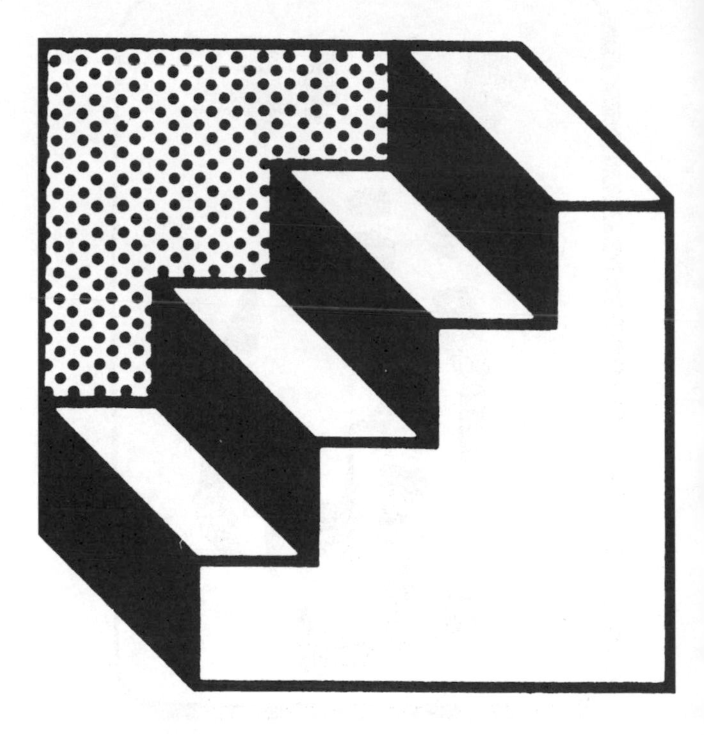

Is this a flight of stairs or a piece of overhanging wall cut to step shape?

Can you spot the dog? What is he an example of?

chump

a. What is special about the word "chump" when written in script?

b. If you say good-bye to Saturn – and head out, what do you say hello to?

Which way are the planks facing?

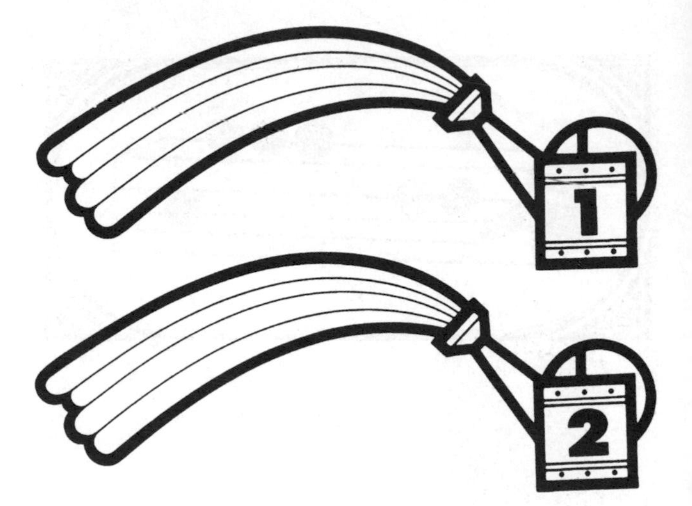

Which water jet is bigger?

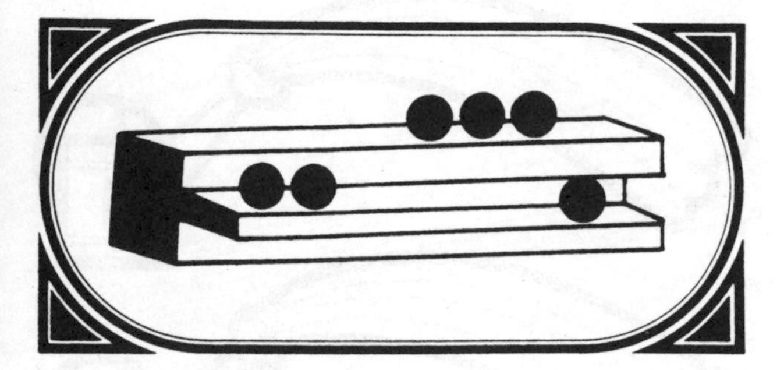

What's wrong with this shelf?

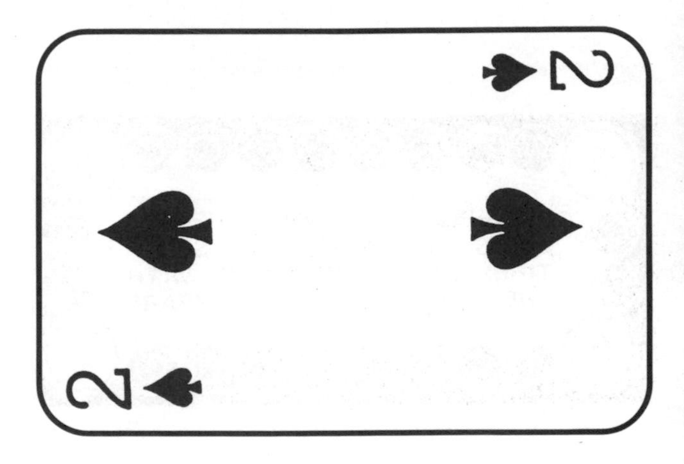

Hold the book in your right hand about five inches in front of you. Close your left eye and focus your right eye on the left pip (the spade symbol). What happens?

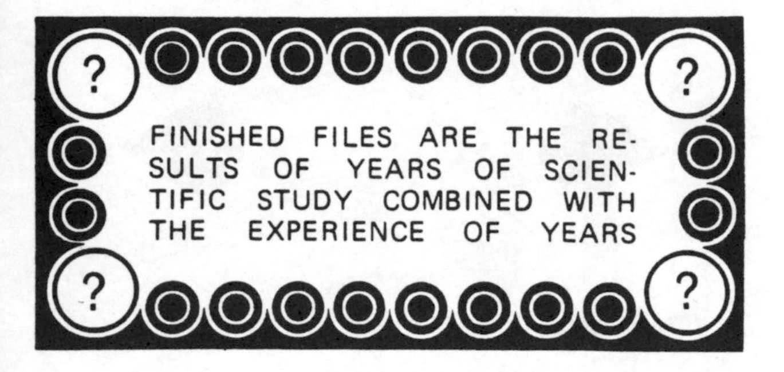

Using only your eyes, count the number of letter "F"s in the above sentence.

Place a small mirror on the center line and look into it to see a word. Why does this work?

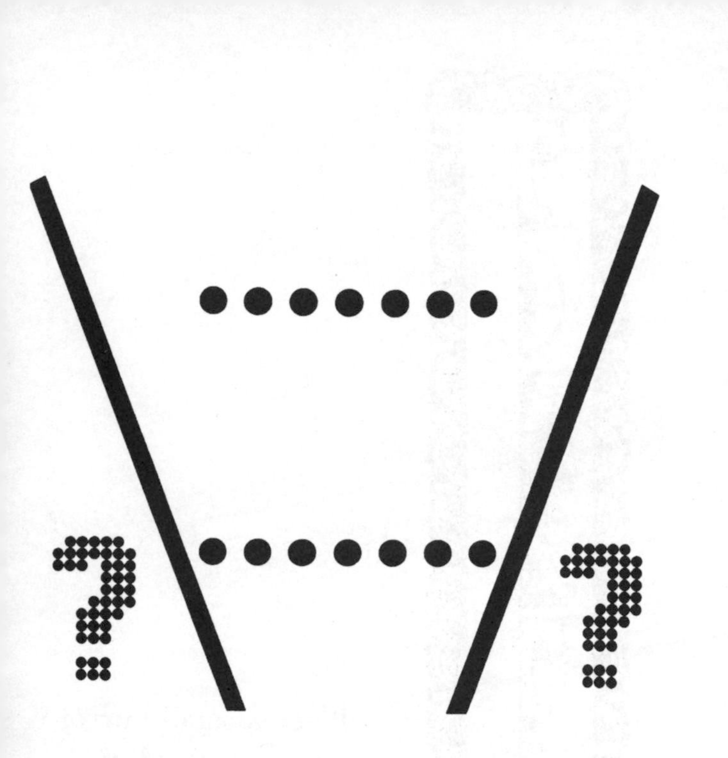

Which of these two horizontal rows of dots is longer?

This picture was taken from a comic strip that appeared in the early part of this century. It was drawn by Gustave Verbeek. Turn the page upside down and what happens?

Stare at the dot for about 30 seconds and try not to blink. Then look at a blank wall or a sheet of white paper, and you will see famous lady. Who is she?

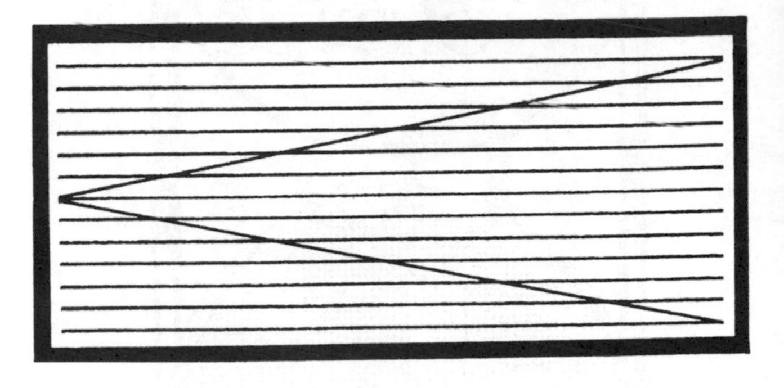

When a single line crosses a grating of parallel lines at an angle of less than 45 degrees, what happens?

Read the words in the hourglass. What do they say? Are you sure?

Which of these two piles of disks is equal in height and width?

Can you decipher the Mandarin's scroll?
Clue: It has to do with playing cards.

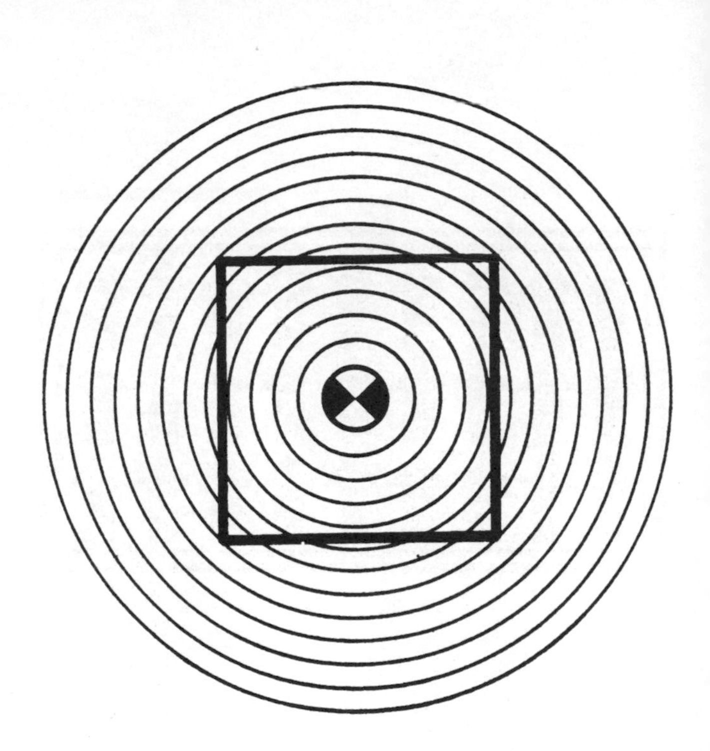

What's wrong with the square?

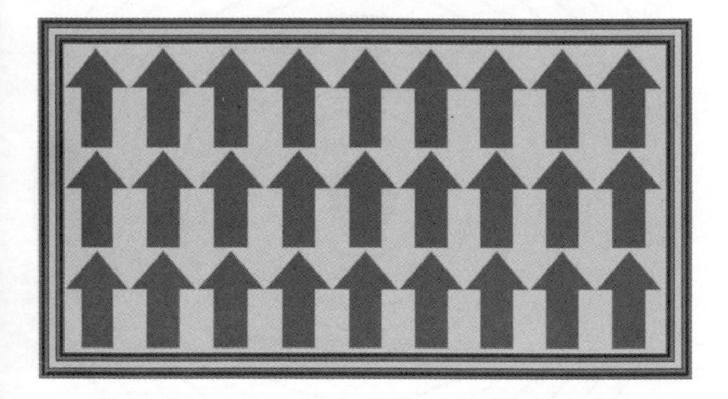

Which is it – dark arrows pointing upwards or light arrows pointing downwards?

Which way are the tubes facing?

This soldier is looking for his horse. Any idea where it is?

Using a mirror, turn this page upside down and look at the reflection of the letters. It's odd that all the words in the black panels can be read easily – but not those in the white panels. How and why do you think this happens?

What is special about this diagram?

Are these balls the same size?

Meet Barnacle Bill, the old sailor. What did he look like when he was young?

Rotate the page in a circular motion. What happens?

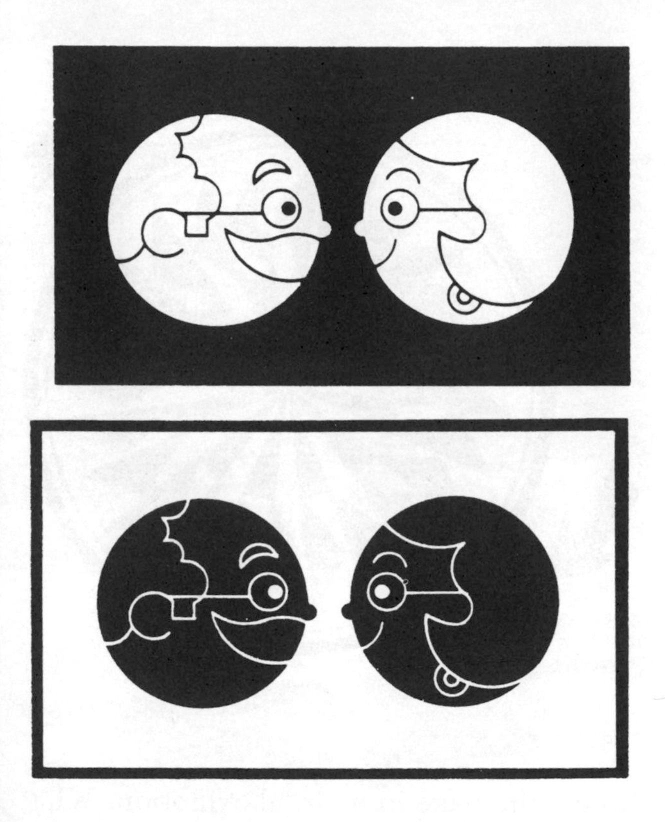

Which set of faces is larger?

This flag was adopted by Canada in 1965.
Can you find the faces in the maple leaf?

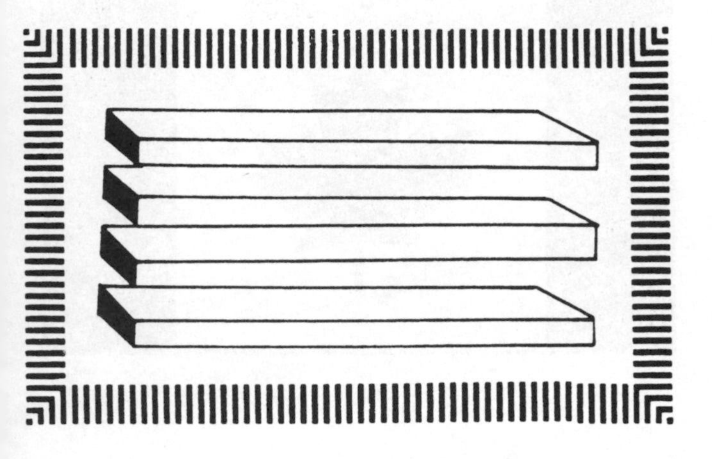

How many planks are there in this picture?

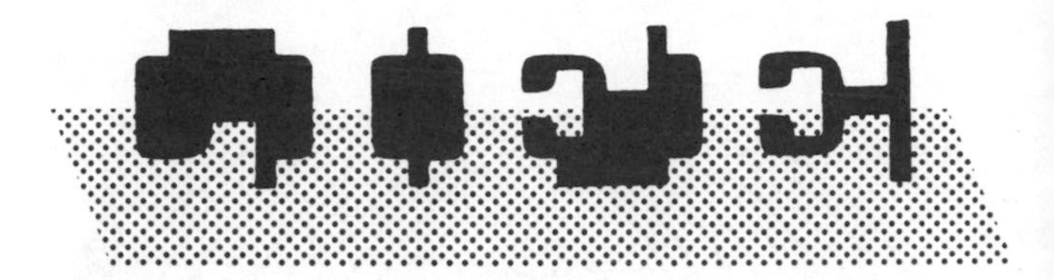

a. Can you work out what these shapes represent?

b. Are these letters upright and parallel?

You can look through this coil from either left or right. Keep staring at it and what happens?

What's the trouble with Grandpa?

Are the horizontal lines straight or crooked?

What is the artist called?

Is this a block with a piece cut out? Or a block with a piece stuck on?

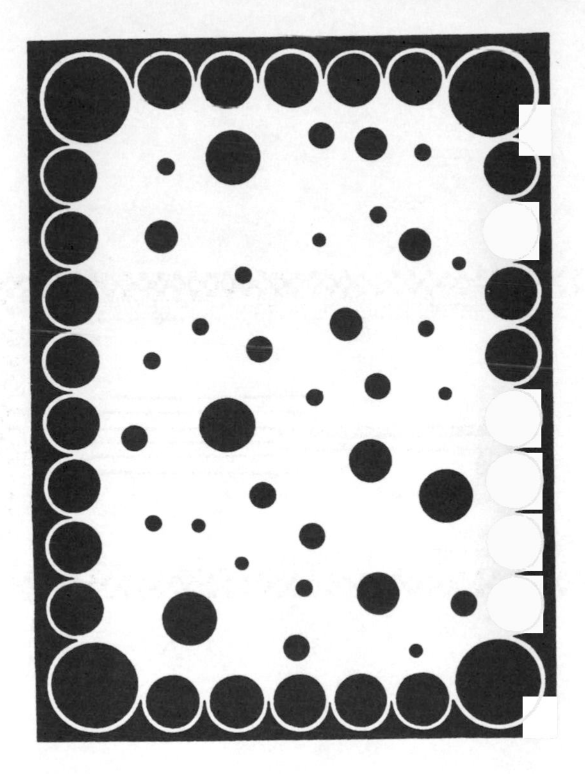

Keep staring at this design under a bright light. After a while, what do you see?

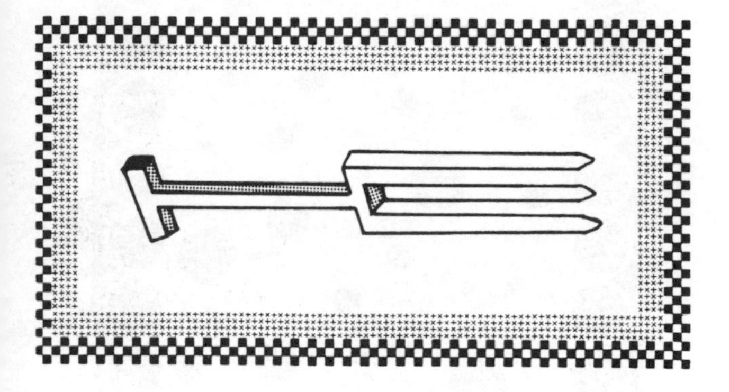

How many prongs are there on this fork?
Do you see two or three?

What's wrong with these fish?

What is this picture?

This sketch is based on "Death and the Bourgeois," which was drawn in the 18th century by Mathaus Merian the Elder. How do you think the painting got its name?

This mathematical problem is wrong. Can you solve it correctly?

Bring this page close to your face, and what happens?

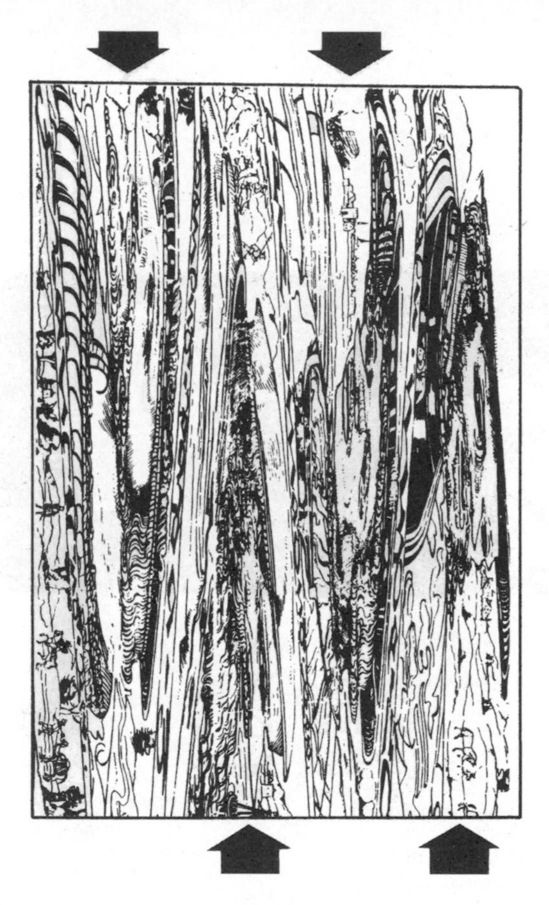

Look at the drawing on page 88. It conceals the heads of four men. It was drawn by Erhard Schon in 1535 and it shows Charles V, Ferdinand I, Pope Paul III, and Francis I. To see the faces, look at the illustration on edge and in the direction of the arrows.

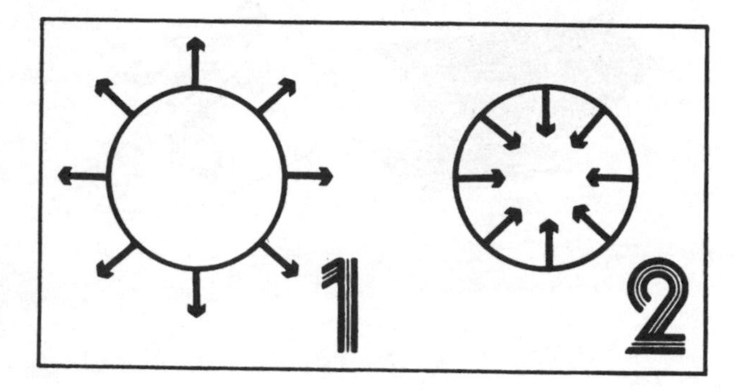

Which circle has the greater diameter – #1 or #2?

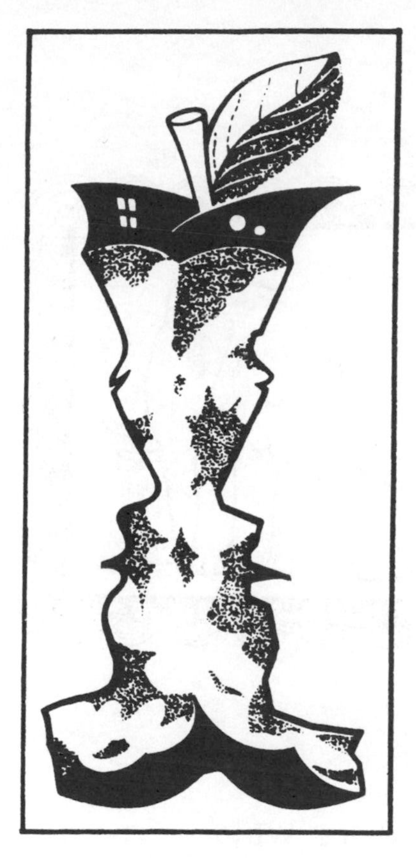

Do you notice anything unusual about this apple core?

This elephant is weird. Why?

Is this clown balancing on a white ball with a black pattern or on a black ball with a white pattern?

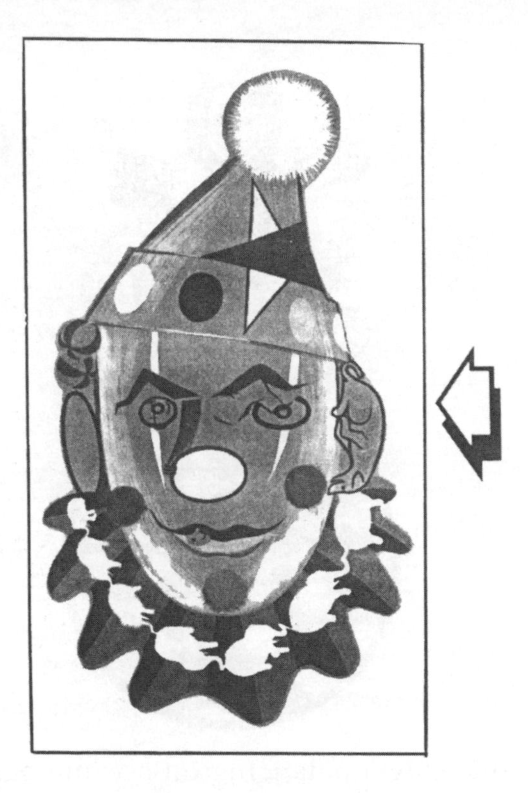

Clowns work in the circus. Here's the clown – where's the circus?

You can make this distorted checkerboard perfectly square without touching it. How?

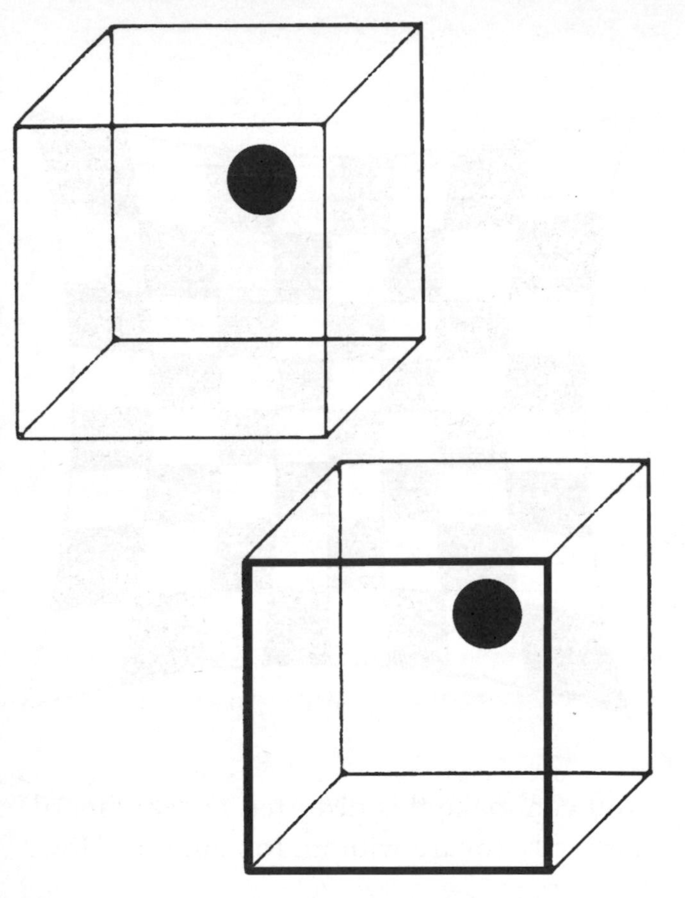

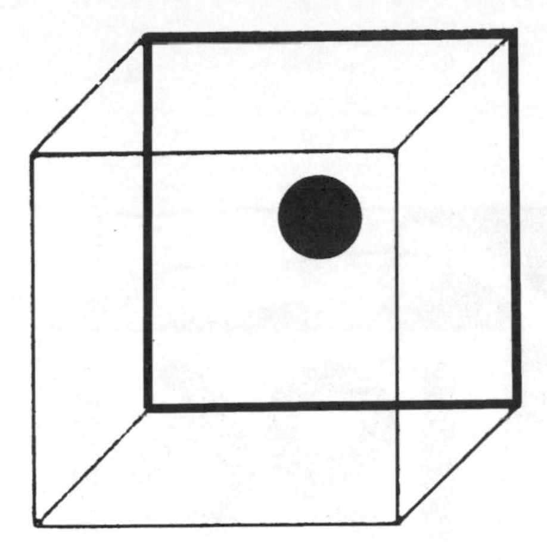

Do you see the area bounded by the darker lines as the outside of a transparent cube? Keep looking, and the bounded area will become the inner surface of a cube tilted a different way. Is the black spot on the front or rear face? Or is it inside the cube?

Turn the year 1961 upside down and it still will say 1961. Turn the page around and see. When will the next "upside down" year occur?

Read this well known phrase. What does it say? Are you sure?

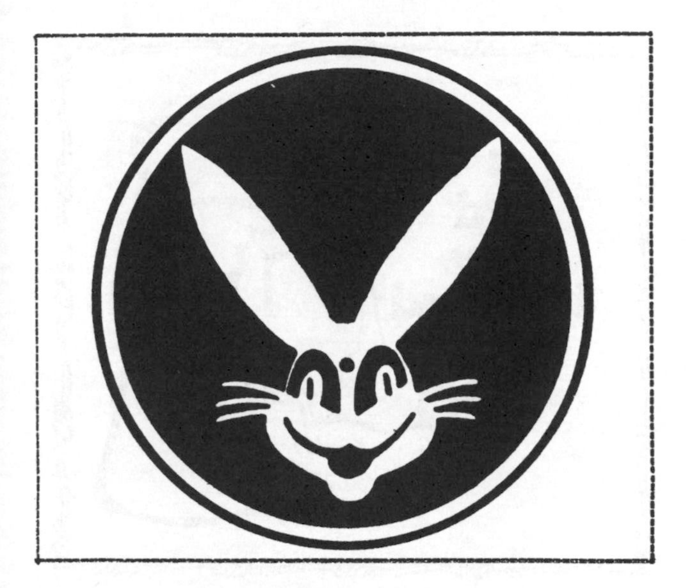

Stare at the dot between the rabbit's eyes (try not to blink). Count slowly to 30. Now look at a piece of white paper or a blank wall. What do you see?

This sketch was first published in 1915. It was drawn by W.E. Hill. It's also known as the "Boring Figure." It shows an old lady and a young woman. Can you find both of them?

This man is looking into a mirror, but something is very odd. Any ideas? How would you explain it? This illustration is based on "La Reproduction Interdite" by Magritte.

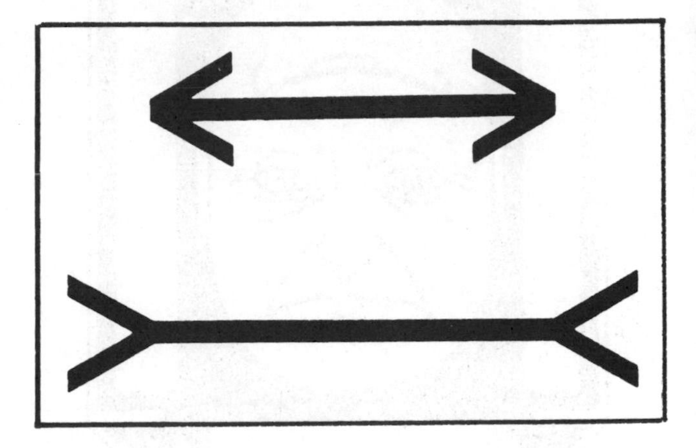

Which line is longer?

Tell this sad fellow a joke and make him smile. Come to think of it, there may be an easier way...

Rotate this page in a counterclockwise direction. What happens?

Which of the two small squares is larger?

Is Side "A" of this picture high or is Side "B"?

What do you see in this picture?

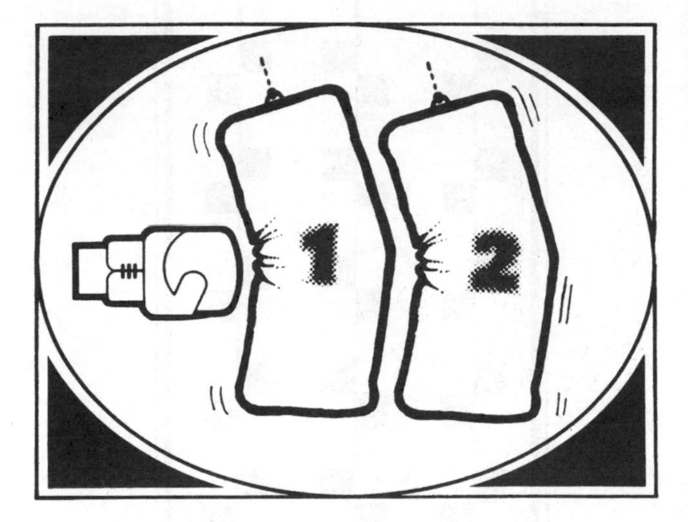

Which punching bag is bigger?

Are these vertical lines straight?

Is this a spiral?

What's the matter with these cubes?

What do you see in this Victorian print?

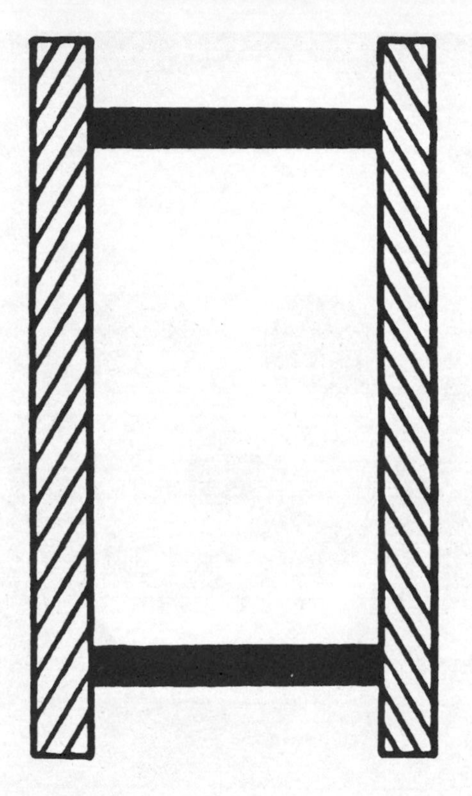

Are these two striped bars closer together at the bottom than at the top?

Can you find the Old Man of the Hills?

This math problem is wrong. Can you find the correct answer?

What's fishy about these fish?

Why is this sketch called “Before and After Marriage”?

a What is going on in this picture?

b And what is this?

What do you see in this picture – black arrows or white arrows?

Why do the fish in this illustration seem to swim in one direction and then in the other?

Look carefully at this dog. Can you find its master?

Is this square tapering off at the right?

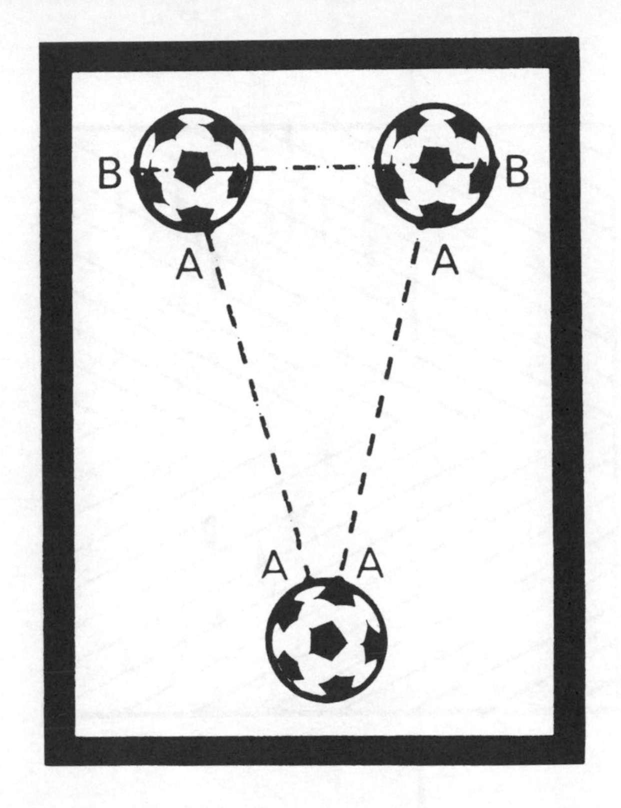

Which distance is greater – "A-A" or "B-B"?

This fairy princess has had a face lift.
What did she look like before?

What do you see in this picture?

Has this triangle been drawn correctly?

What do you make out of the design on page 129? To find out, tilt the page to eye level as in the sketch above. What words do you see?

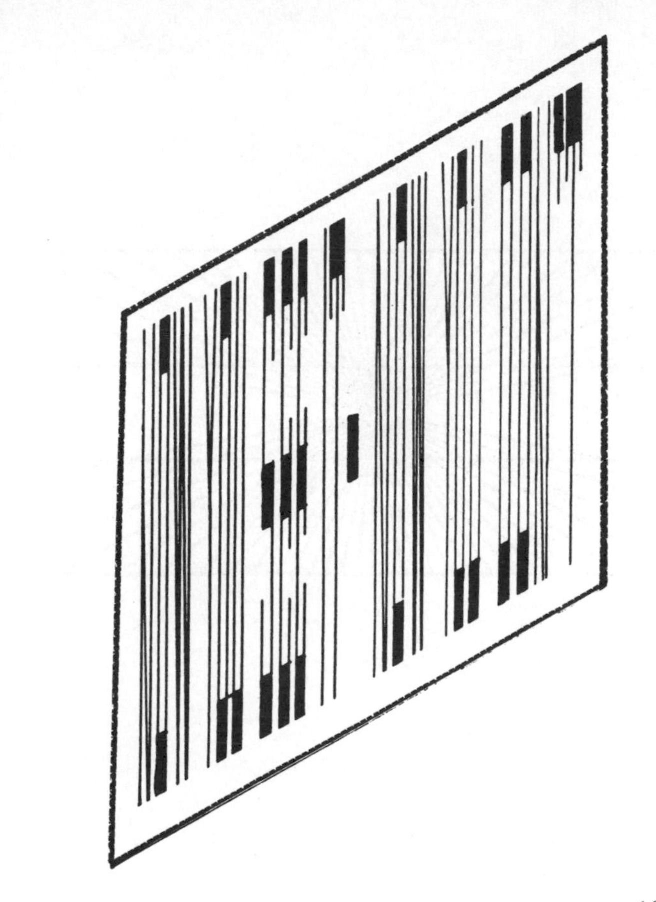

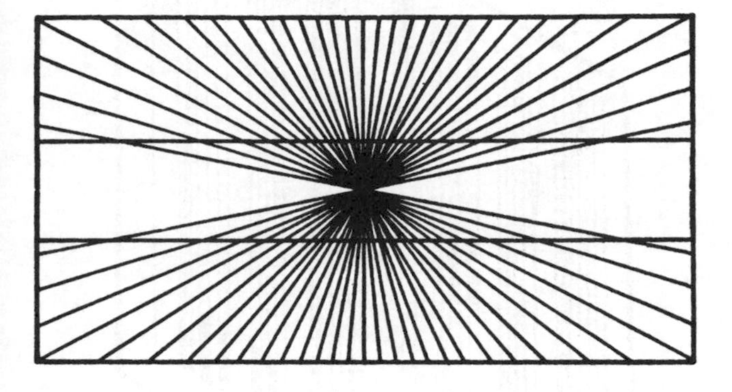

Are the horizontal lines straight?

What do you see in this picture?

What is this sign painter painting? Two young women with beards? Or a large puppy?

Are Abraham Lincoln and Ben Franklin looking in different directions?

Which bridge is the biggest?

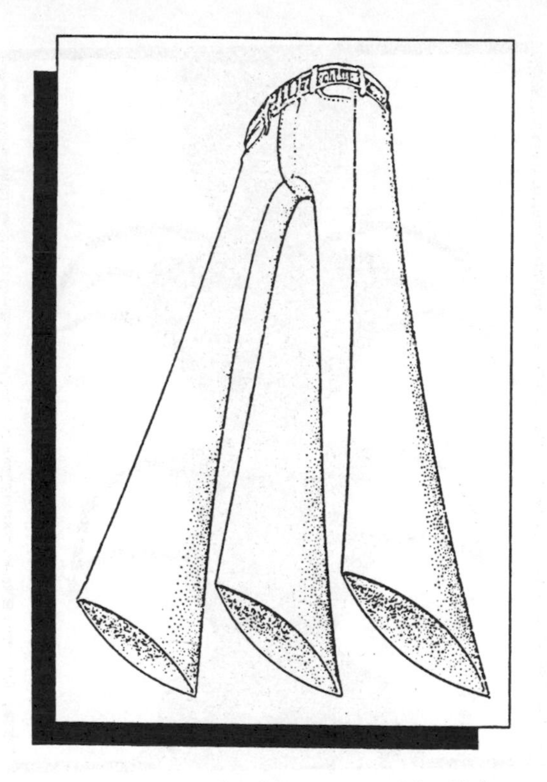

What's wrong with this pair of bell-bottom pants?

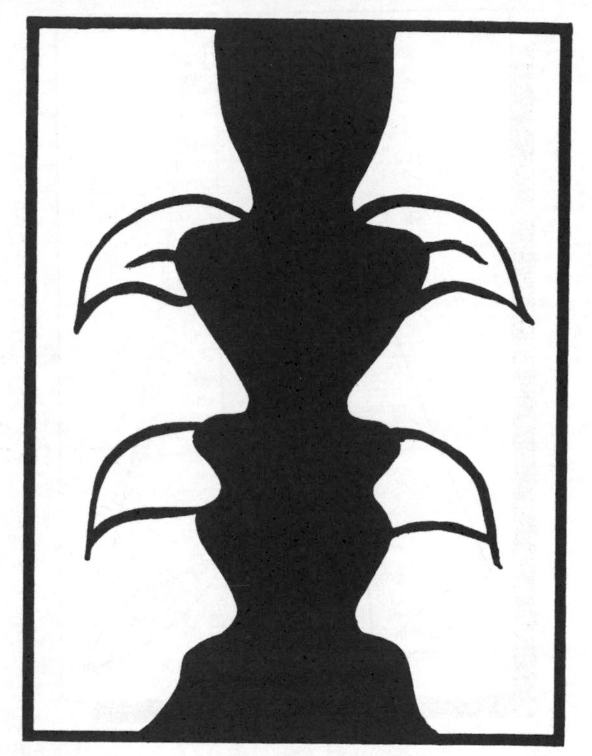

Is this a strange plant or two faces looking at each other?

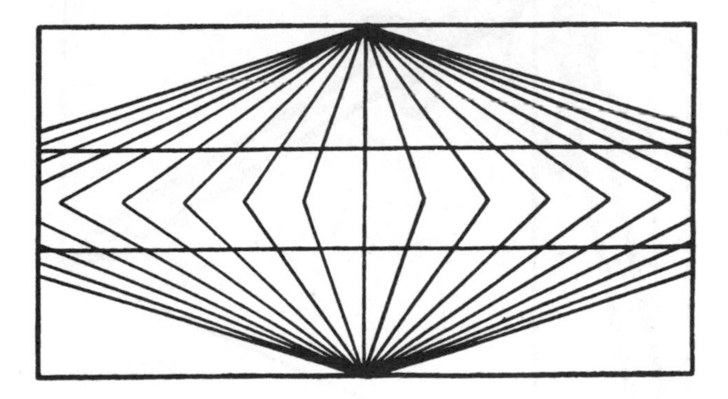

Are the two horizontal lines bending in towards each other?

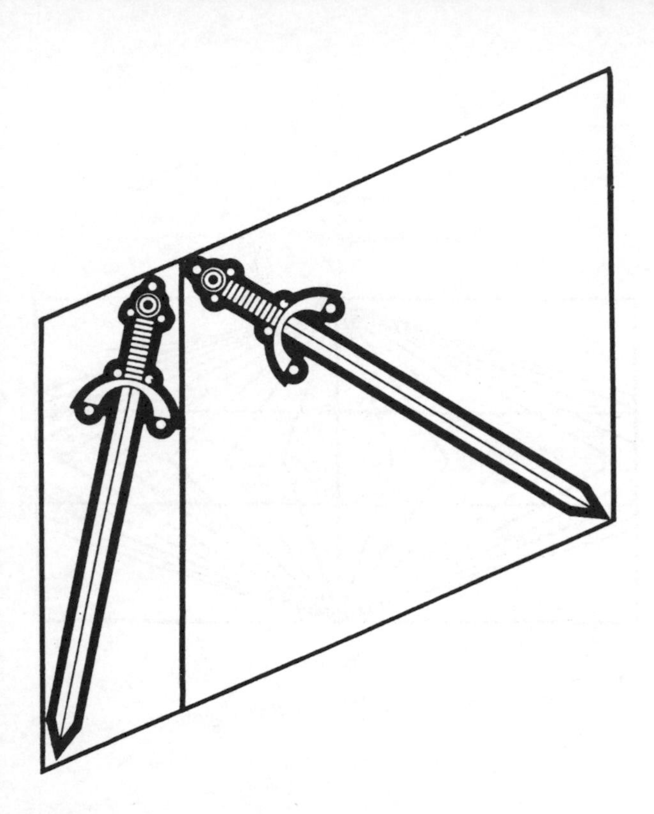

These two swords have been drawn in a parallelogram. Which looks bigger?

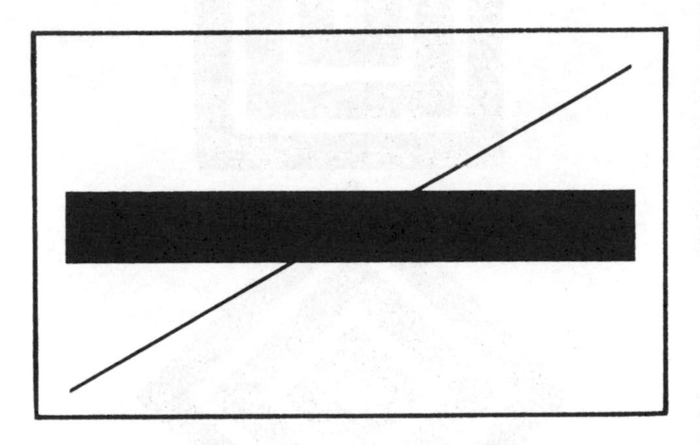

Is the upper thin diagonal line lined up directly with the lower diagonal line?

Which square is bigger?

Which dot is on the inside?

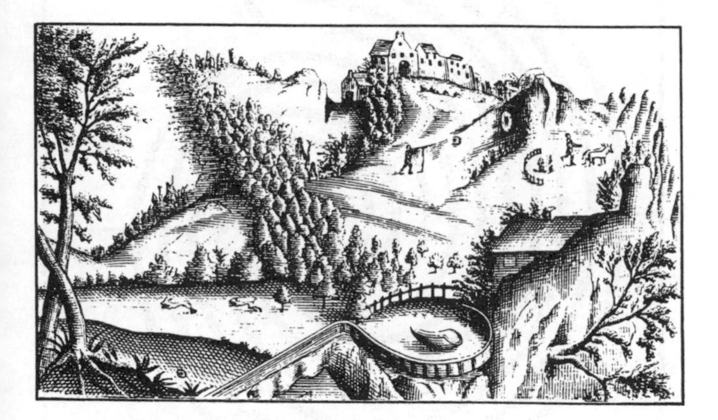

Where is the farmer hiding?

Cinderella is sad because she wants to go to the ball. Her Fairy Godmother can make her wish come true. Where is this magic lady?

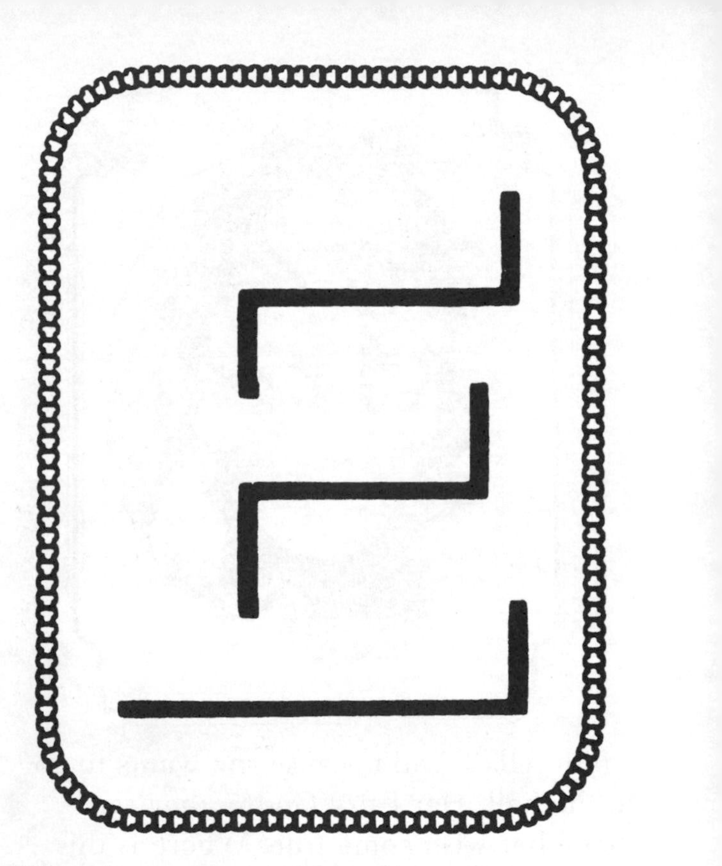

What do you see in this picture?

This fat man has been eating too much.
What will happen if he goes on eating?

Is this a solid figure with one long edge? Or do you see it as two solid figures leaning on each other?

Do you see white arrows or black arrows?

How do you turn a duck into a rabbit?

Is this 3 black squares in a white square – or is it something else?

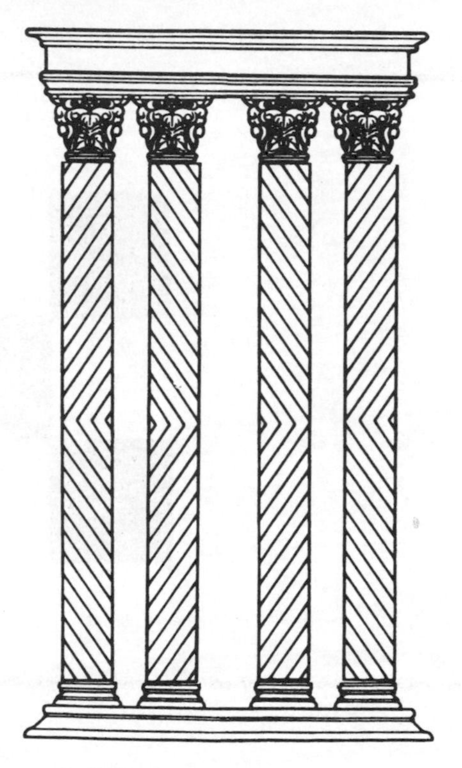

Are these columns about to buckle and fall down?

Are the 3 dots on the inside or on the outside of this impossible frame?

What are the 4 pictures on page 153?

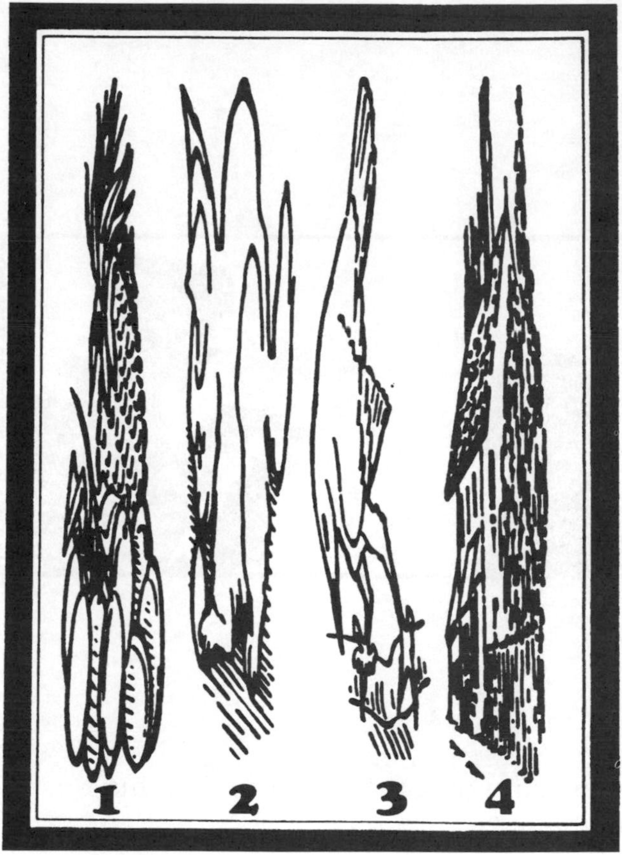

1 2 3 4

How can you get this kid to take his medicine?

A clown and a ball. Can you figure out how to make the ball spin?

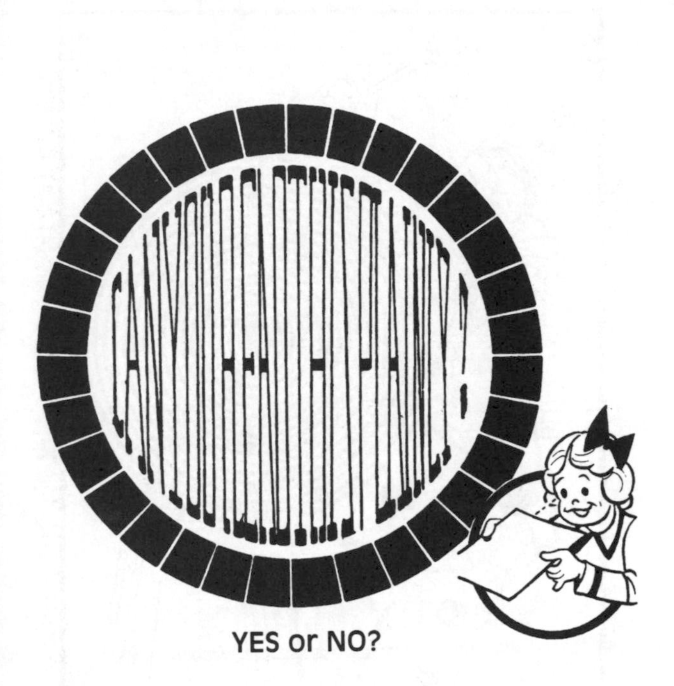

Can you read the hidden message? And is the answer yes or no?

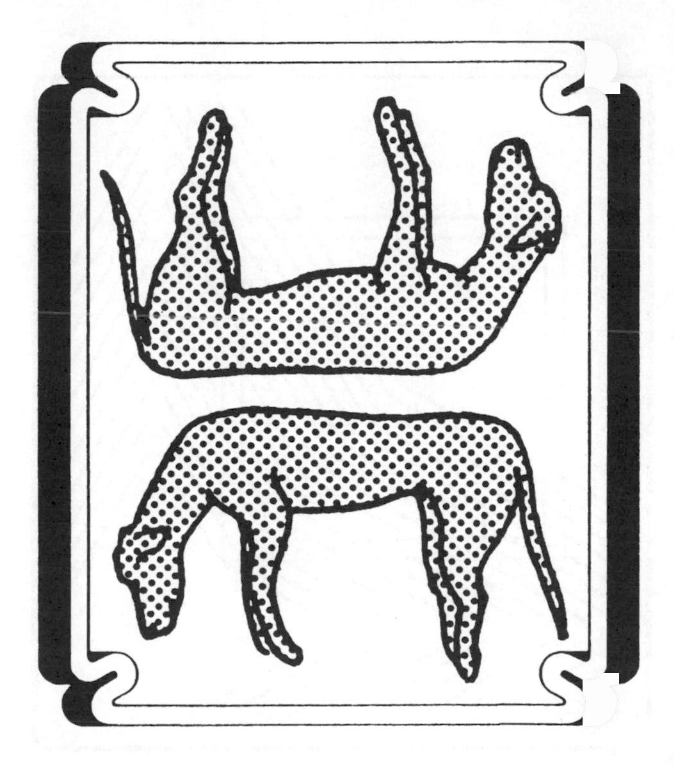

These 2 dogs are dead – or are they? How can you bring them back to life?

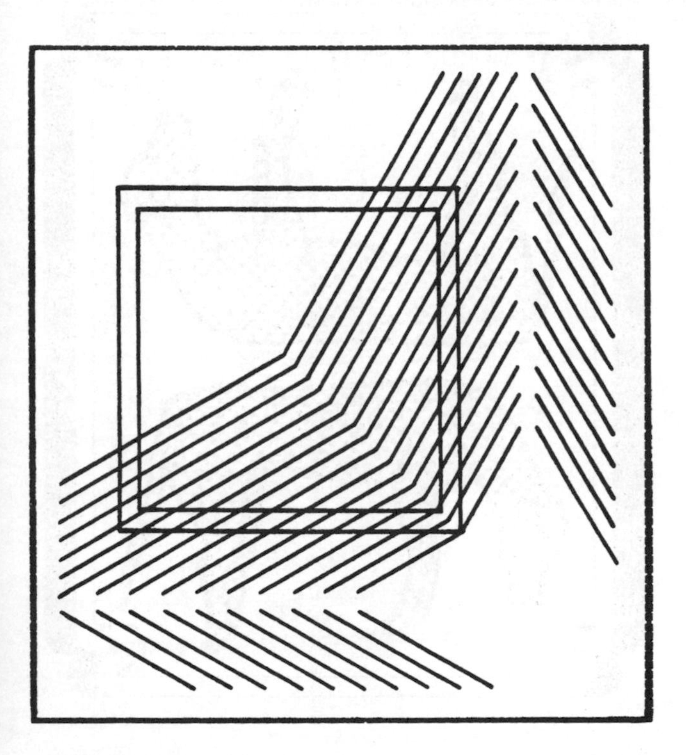

What's making this square look so weird?

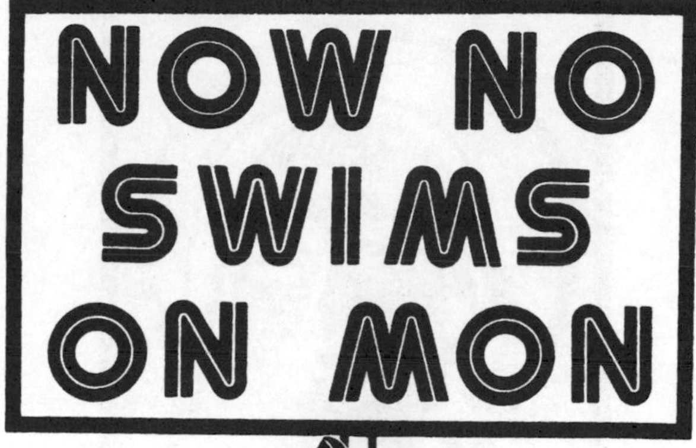

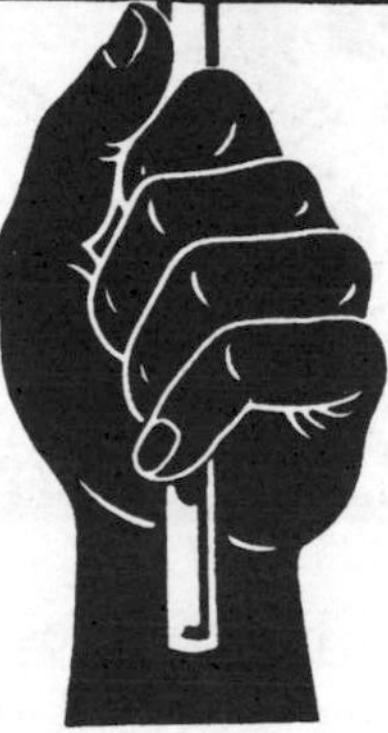

What is unusual about this sentence?

Stare at this old French design for about 30 seconds under a bright light (try not to blink). Then look at a blank wall or a piece of white paper. What do you see?

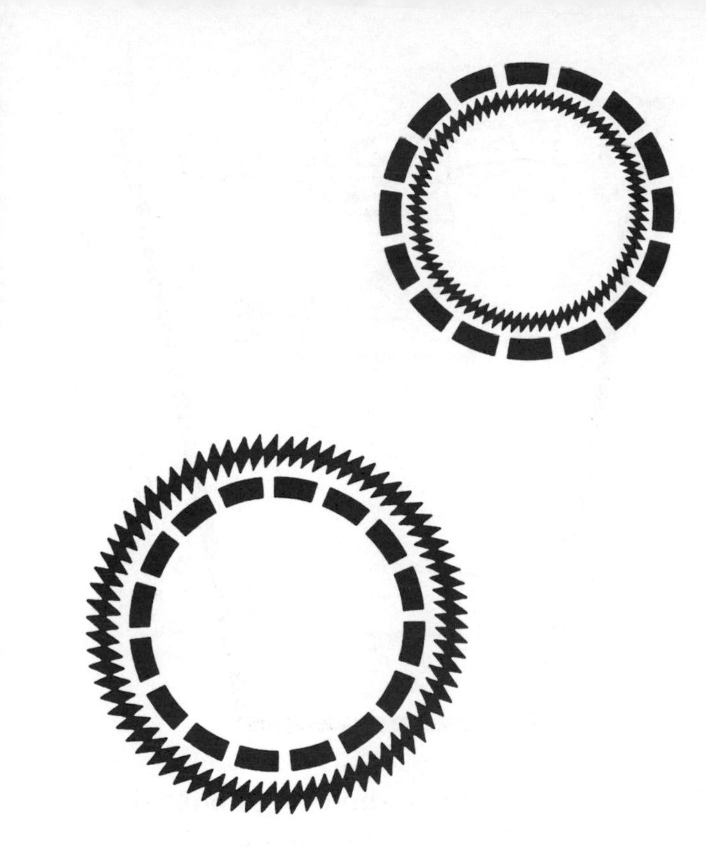

Which broken circle is bigger?

Fishermen are always boasting about the size of the fish they have caught. This man has caught 2 fish. Which one is bigger?

This man is unhappy because his girlfriend has left him. What does she look like?

What happens when you rotate this page in a circular motion?

a. Stare at the center of the illustration and then slowly bring the page towards your face. What happens to this couple?

b. Can you figure out what these shapes represent?

This bald-headed old soldier looks rather weird. What do you think he looked like when he was a child?

These black and white tiles look uneven. They certainly are not in straight lines – or are they?

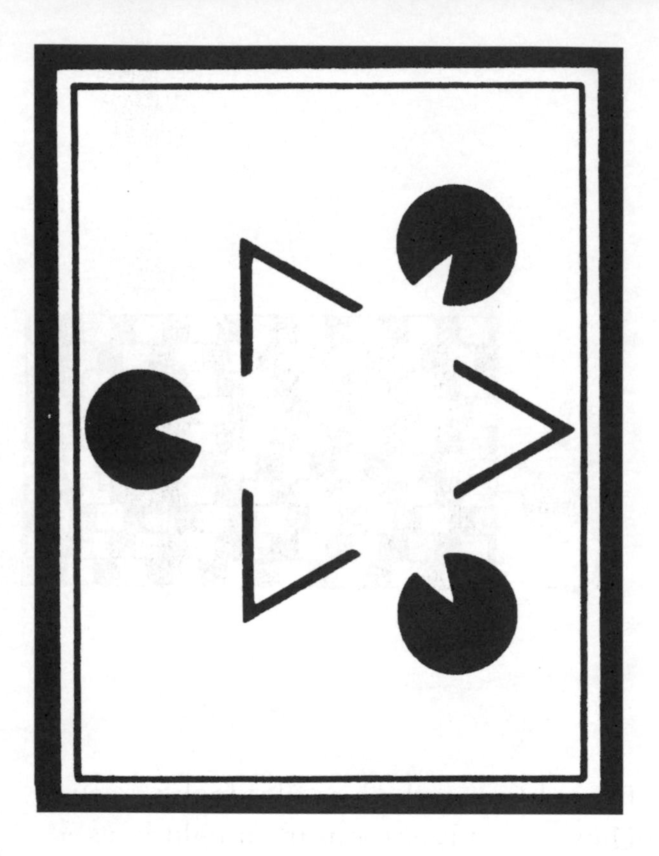

Can you see the white triangle?

This 18th-century engraving was created by William Hogarth. It may be the original "What's Wrong with This Picture?" picture. How many "absurdities" of perspective do you think there are in this scene–10? 20? 30?

How many blocks do you see in this picture? Six or seven?

It's hard work digging clay.
Save it for a rainy day.

a. What's the last word of each sentence?

b. What creates the illusion of movement in this picture?

Meet the Man in the Moon. If you add a few lines to his face, it will change into two faces. Can you guess where to put the lines?

This portrait was first published in Rome around the year 1585. What else is special about it?

What does it say in the center box?

Are the rings in this “flip-flop” design pointing up to the left or down to the right?

You've seen this illusion many times. It can be either a vase or two faces looking at each other. What is it called?

This is an amazing frog. When confronted with any sort of danger, it changes into a horse. Try looking at this sketch from different angles. Can you find the horse?

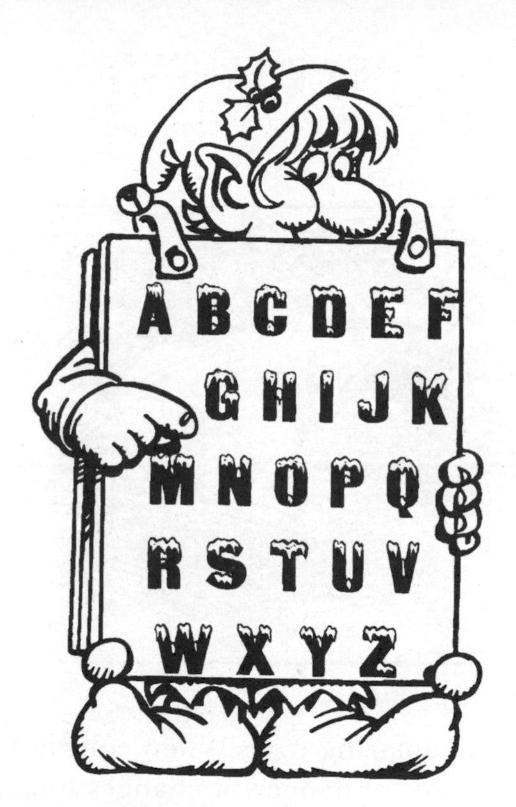

What Christmas greeting is conveyed by these letters?

The name of this picture is “Time Passes.” What is special about it?

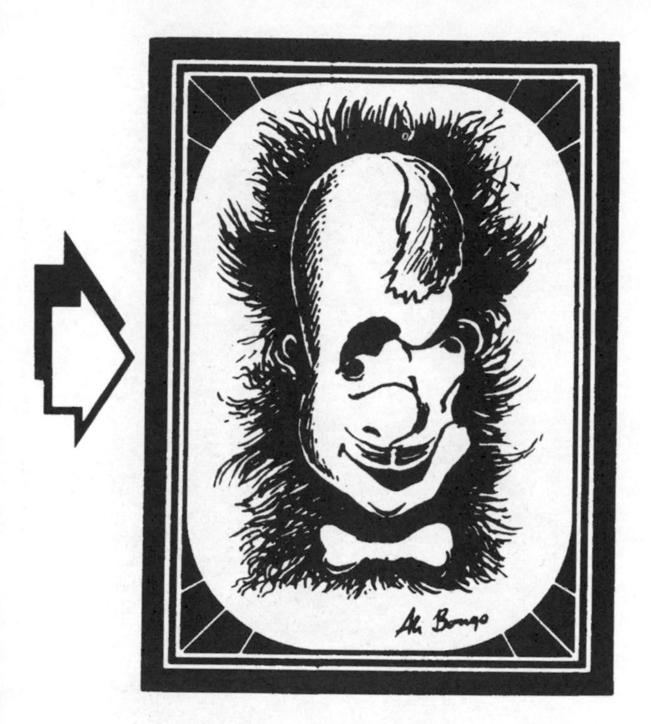

Can you make out what this is–animal, vegetable, or mineral? Try looking at it from different angles.

Do you see this as 4 chevrons (badges, like stripes on a uniform)? Or as the sides of 4 cubes?

What is your first impression of this silhouette?

A farmer put this sign up. Can you understand what he was trying to say?

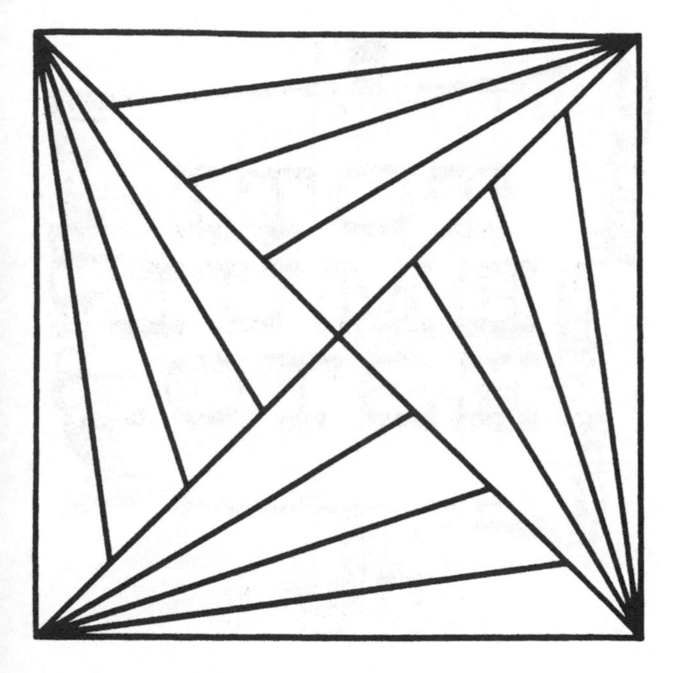

How many triangles can you find in this design?

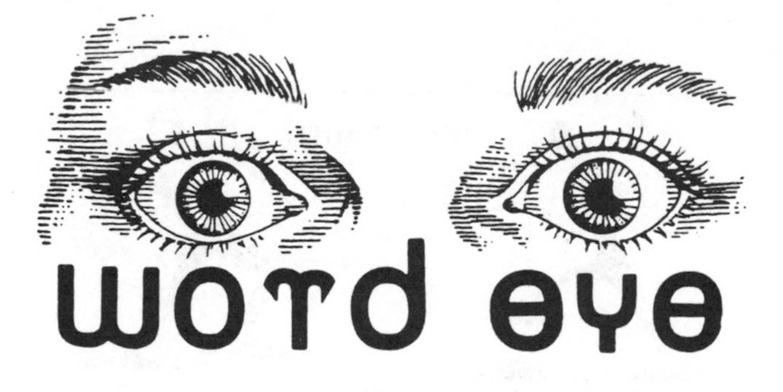

Look at the reflection of this picture in a mirror. You will see a word that is connected with your eyes. What is it?

Bring this page close to your face, and what happens?

Can you find the captain of this ship?

Are these columns narrower at the top?

The rear view of a young woman. Look carefully and you may see something else. What is it?

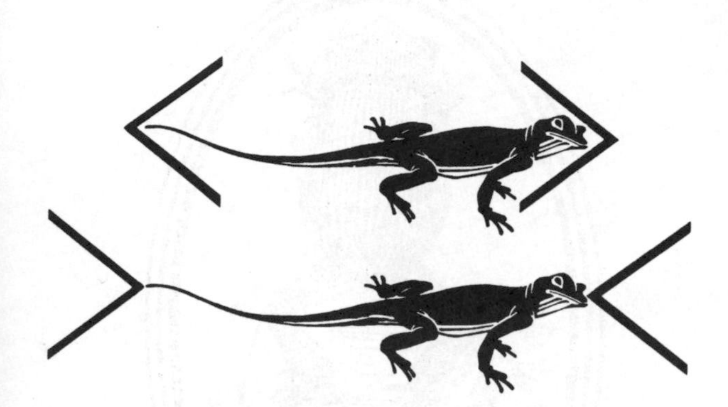

a. Which lizard is longer?

b. The heart is closer to which end of the line?

Move this page closer to your face. What is going to happen to this little character?

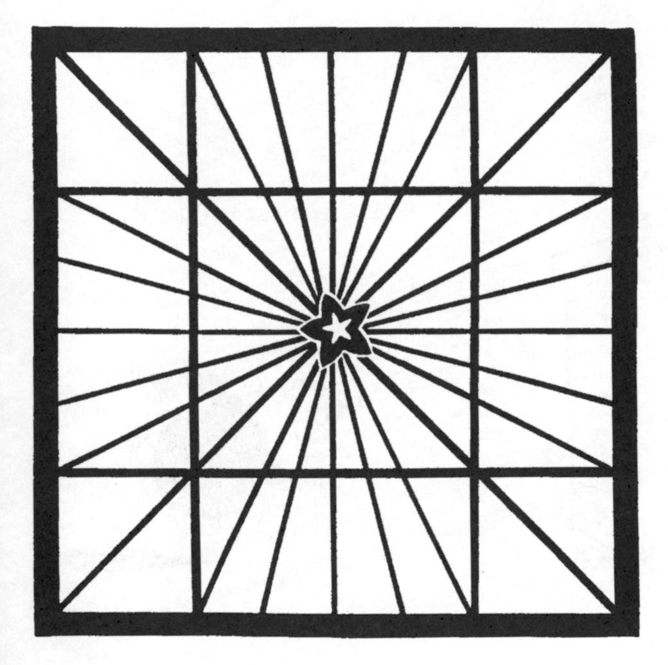

Is the middle square bulging out?

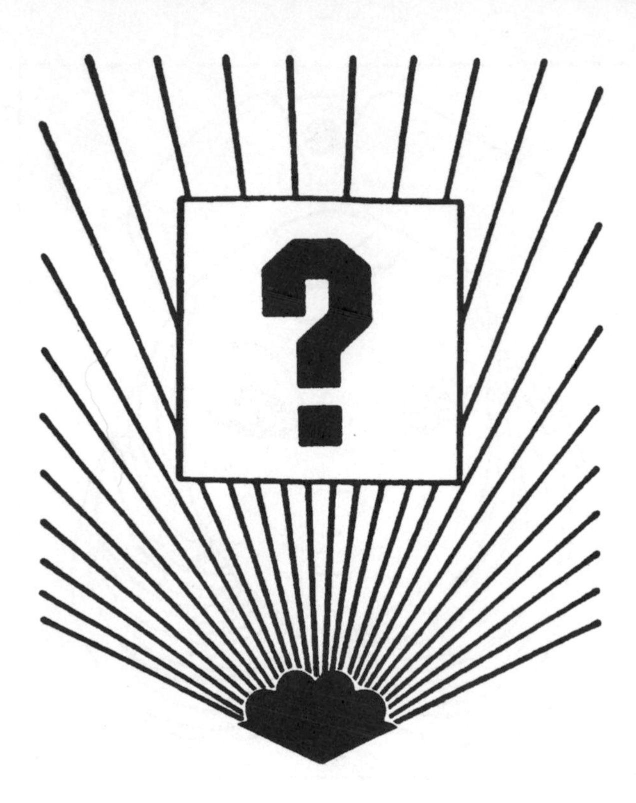

How about this square? Is it narrower on top?

This nurse is at work. But where is her patient?

Can you find the wife of the fellow in this old French illustration?

What is unusual about this picture?

This student was very bright. Years later he became a professor. What do you think he looks like now?

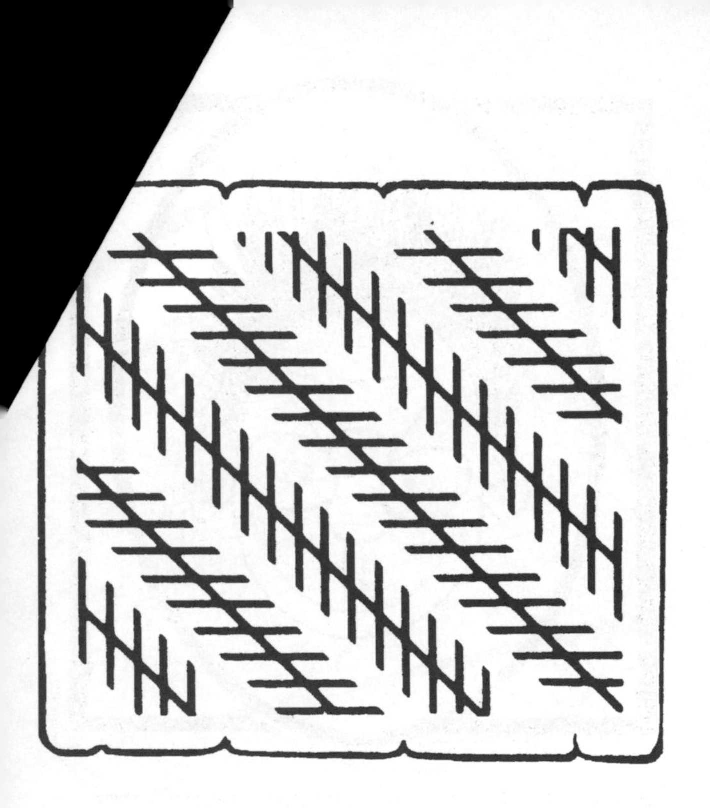

Are these long diagonal lines straight?

What's wrong with the small circle?

Here are a young girl and her grandmother. Can you see them both?

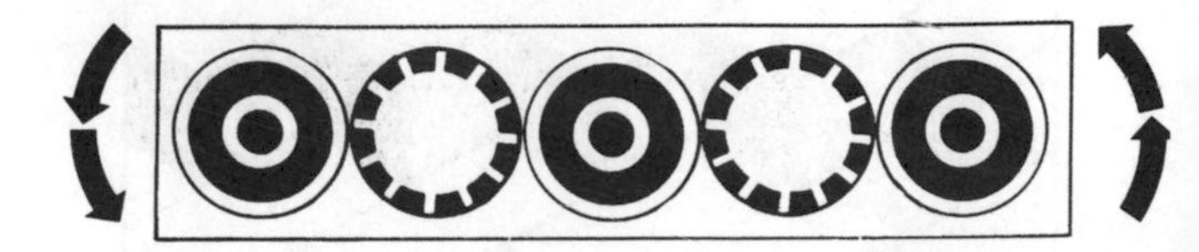

a. Rotate this page in a circular motion in the direction of the arrows. What happens?

b. Can you figure out what these shapes represent?

Is this a stack of bricks pointing down to the right or up to the left?

What's wrong with this spiral?

The soldier in this old French design has a baby. Where is it?

How can you get the bee to move closer to the flower?

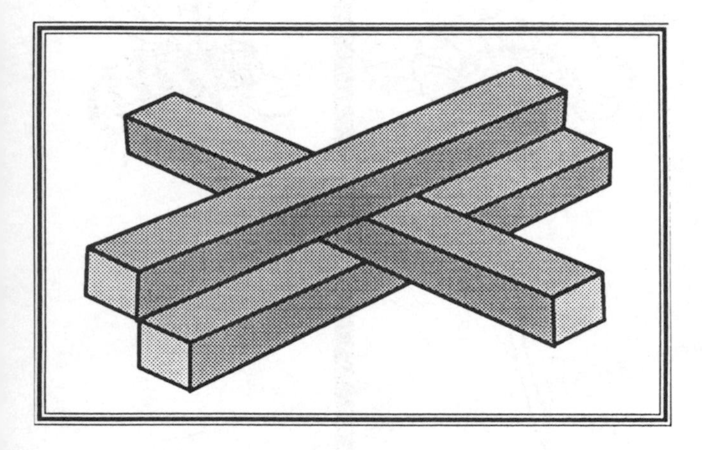

Could you put together this construction out of wood?

What's the title of this book? Are you sure?

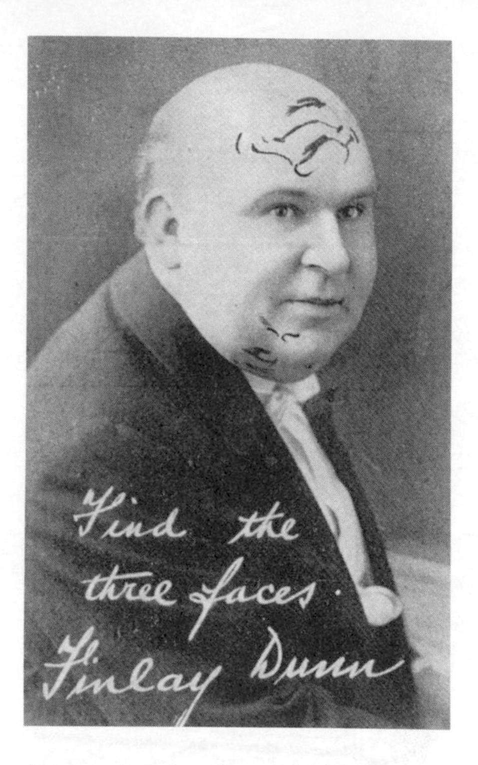

Finlay Dunn had a vaudeville act in England during the early part of the 20th century. Can you find his three faces?

Is this drum a perfect circle?

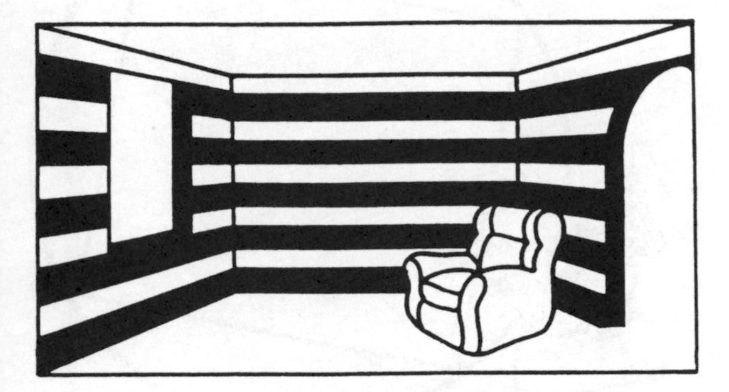

How can you make a room look bigger?

Can you find the cattle rustler who has been hidden in this picture?

This is Farmer Brown's horse Dobbin. Do you see Farmer Brown?

Here is the Gateway Arch in St. Louis. Is it taller than it is wide?

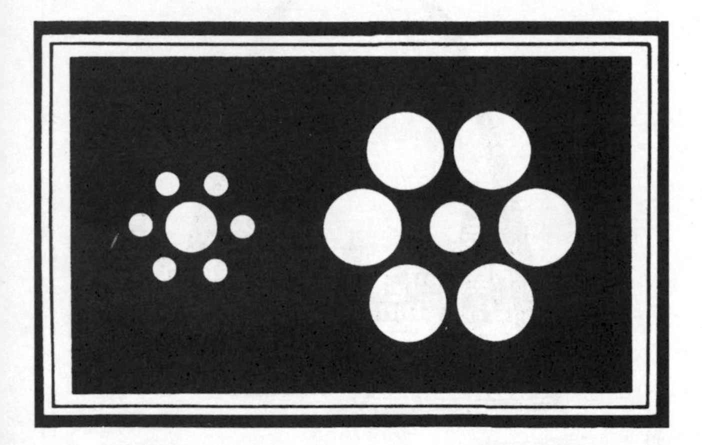

The center of one of the flowers looks bigger than the other. Is it really bigger?

Can you see where the criminal is hiding?

Do you see this as two faces or a lighted candle?

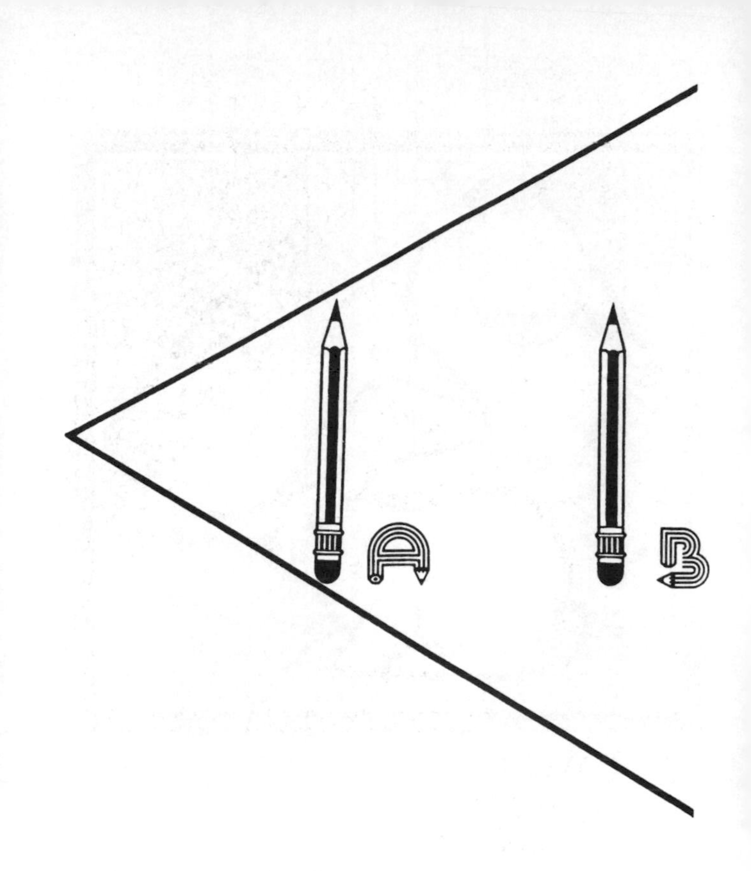

Which pencil is bigger?

What's the matter with these rabbits?

Stare at the cross for about 30 seconds. Then look at a blank wall or a piece of white paper, and what do you see?

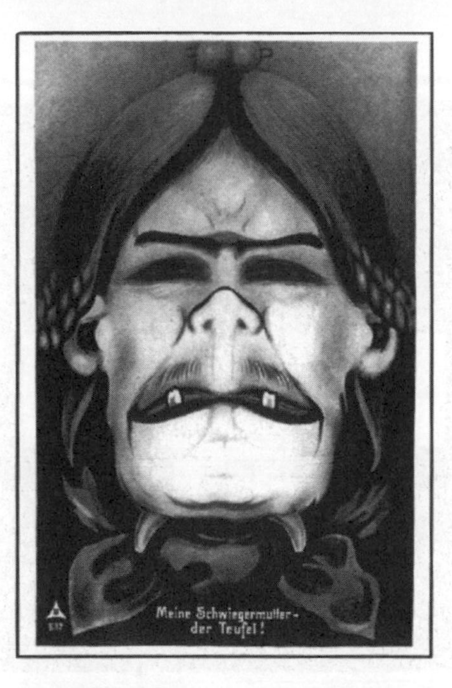

This gruesome picture comes from the end of the 19th century. The caption says "My mother in law–the devil." Why do you think it says that?

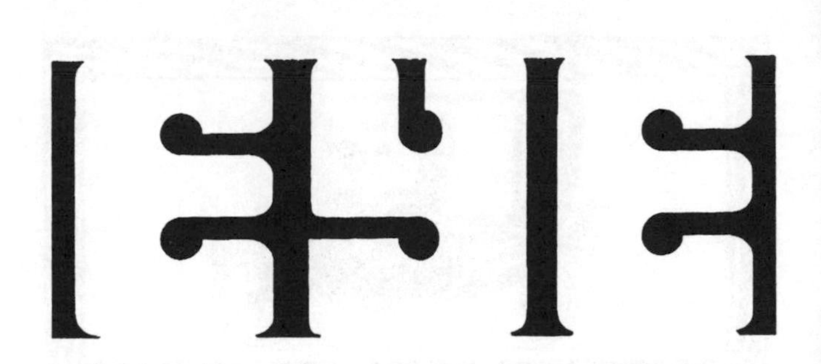

What are these black symbols?

Is this picture frame narrower at the right-hand side?

In this Top Hat illusion, is the brim smaller, the same size, or larger than the height of the hat?

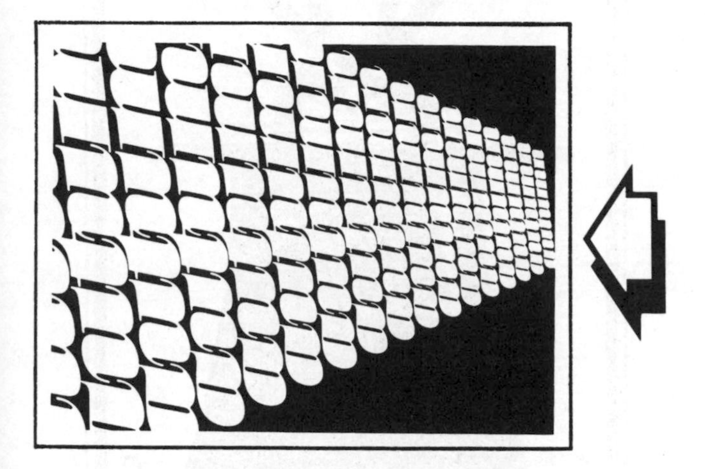

Is this a series of abstract shapes–or a message?

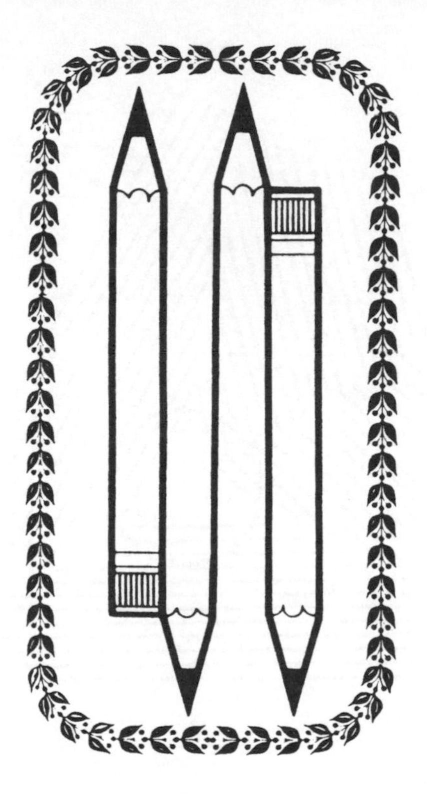

Can you use these disappearing pencils for writing secret messages?

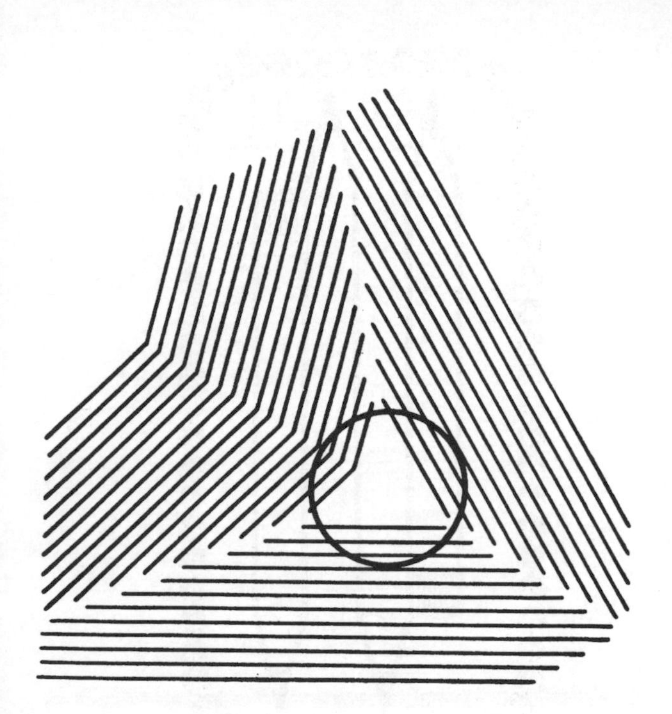

Is this small ring a perfect circle?

Can you read and understand what has been typed?

The soldier is aiming his gun right at you. Move your head from left to right, and what happens?

Here is another very old illustration, of a theme that has been popular over the centuries. You've already seen one of them in this book. Can you figure out what it's about?

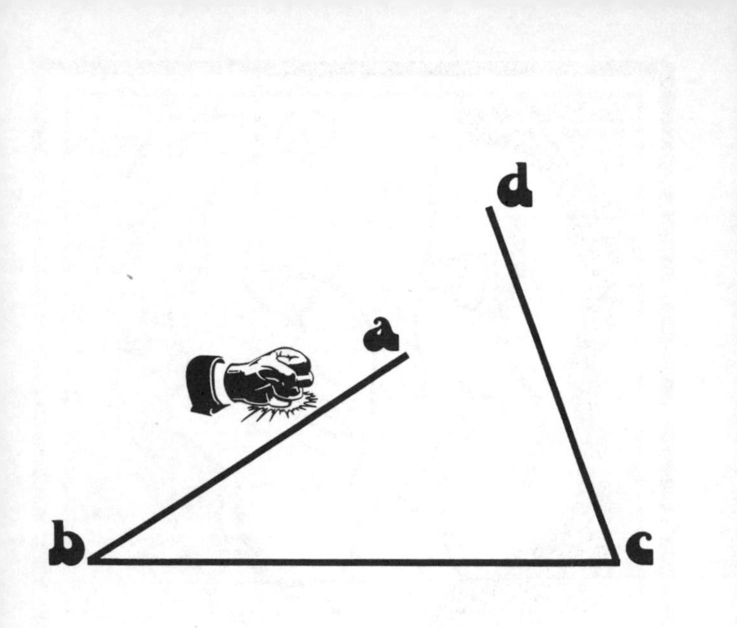

Is line a-b longer than line c-d?

With just one move, can you think of a way of making the matches form a complete oblong shape?

This black and white design seems "higgledy-piggledy," but it is a regular pattern. Hold the page as in the small sketch and look in the direction of the arrow. What happens?

The artist put together a bunch of separate silhouettes in this portrait of Abraham Lincoln. What silhouettes are used?

This portrait is based on a 19th century print. What do you have to do to turn this miserable character into a miserable rabbit?

What do you see in this picture?

This is called "The Man of a Thousand Faces." Can you tell why?

A member of the audience is sleeping. He is hidden in this picture. Can you find him?

Which line connects with "c"?

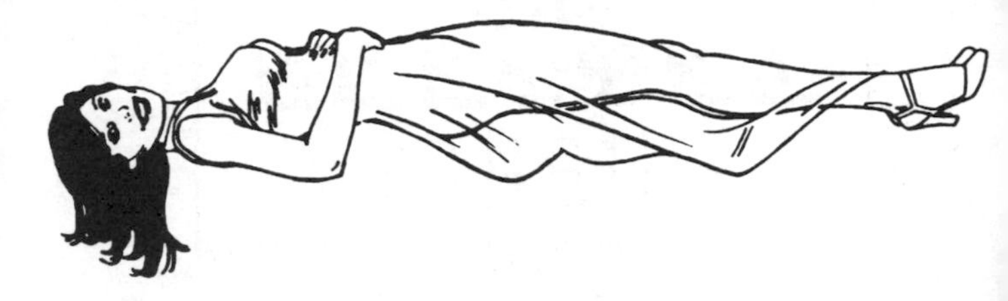

Slowly bring the page close to your face–so that you make the "spot" touch your nose. What happens?

There are no letters in this picture. All the words are made up of "shadow" type characters. So how do we know what this says?

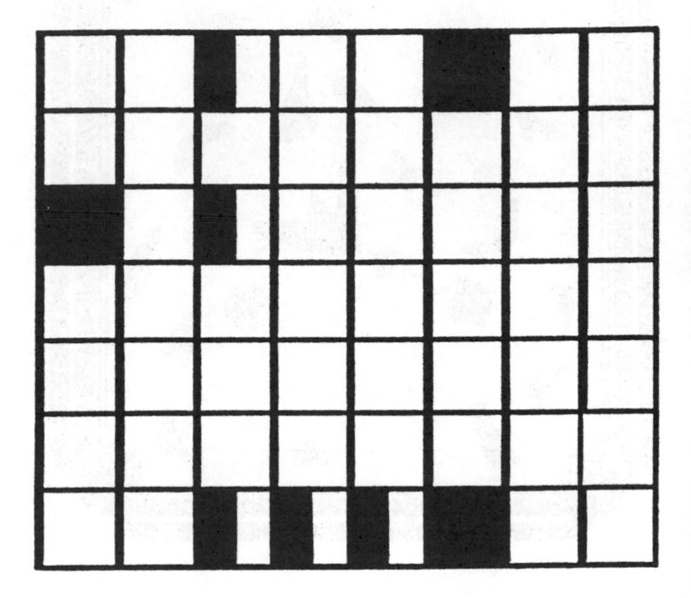

Can you discover this secret message?

The black shapes may seem unrelated, but they go together. This is actually a familiar subject. It is another example of “closure.” Can you figure out what it is?

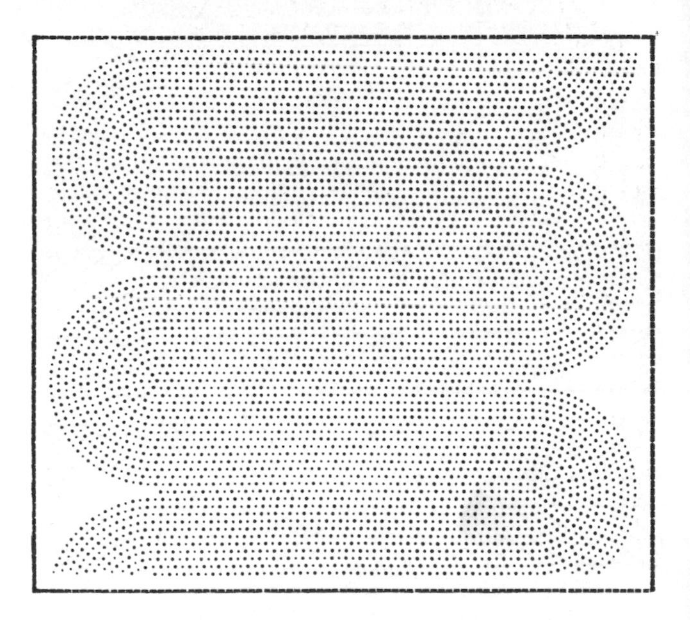

Hundreds of small dots. But look at this page from a distance and what do you see?

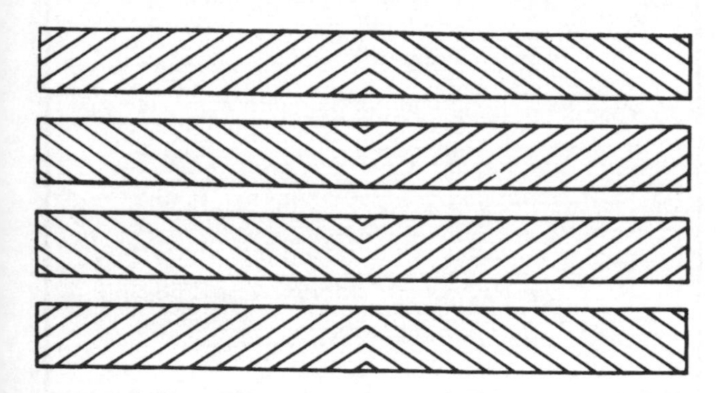

These four planks seem to bend and bow, but do they really?

Can you name the 8 animals that have been hidden in the branches of the trees in this old print?

One morning a digital clock shows readout #1, which is odd, since it's well before noon. Nearly two hours later, the clock shows readout #2. Can you guess what is causing the incorrect displays?

Meet the Bishop—and his brother. Can you tell what his brother's occupation is?

Can you figure out why this logo (designed by Leo Lionni) was used for the 25th anniversary of the Museum of Modern Art?

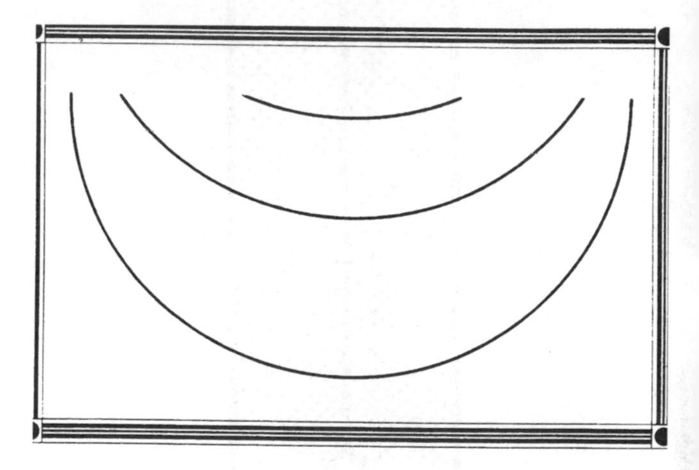

These three arcs are all part of the same circle, but they don't seem to have the same curve. Or do they?

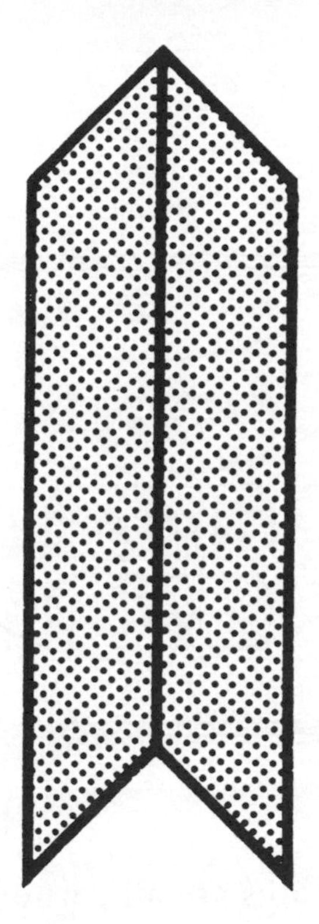

Is this piece of folded card facing toward you or away from you?

What does it say in the center box?

This "Op Art" cube is strange. What is the matter with it?

"The Two Friends" is an old French puzzle. It is a portrait of a lady. Can you find her best friend?

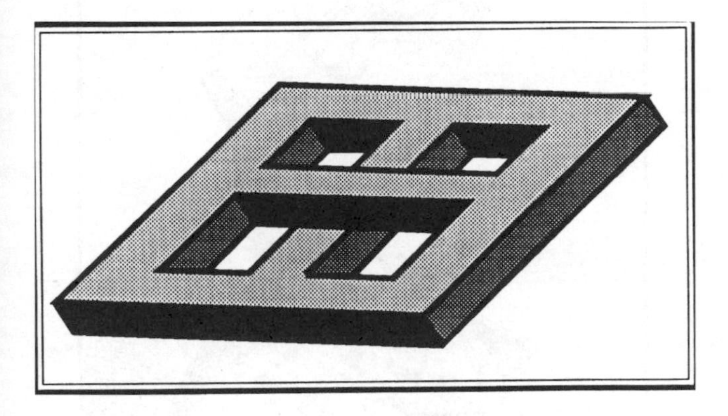

This window frame is easy to draw. Would it be easy to make?

This old-fashioned Valentine contains two secret phrases. What are they?

This illustration dates back to the First World War. The Kaiser is on the run. Who made him run?

Why would anyone use vertical striped wallpaper like the type in this picture?

What happens when you turn this wavy design–of peaks and troughs–upside down?

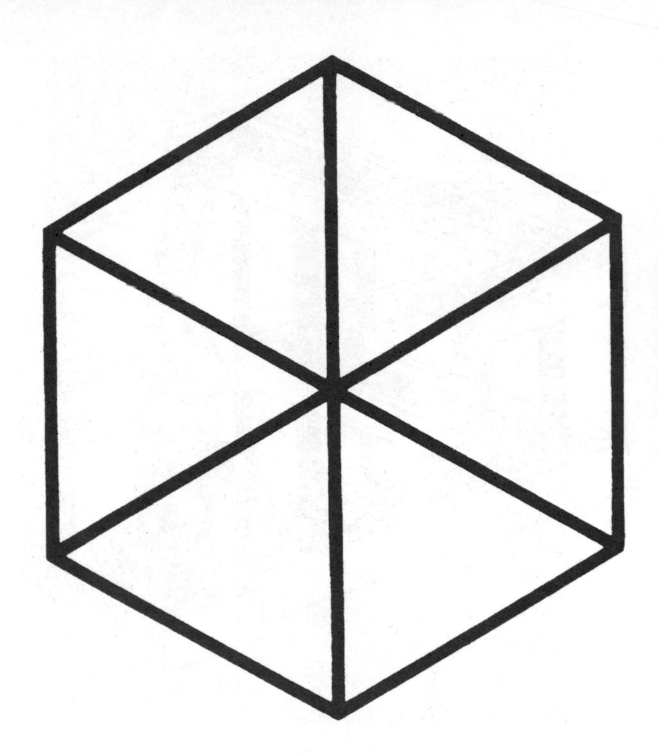

This object is a hexagon. But if you look at it differently, it is also something else. What is it?

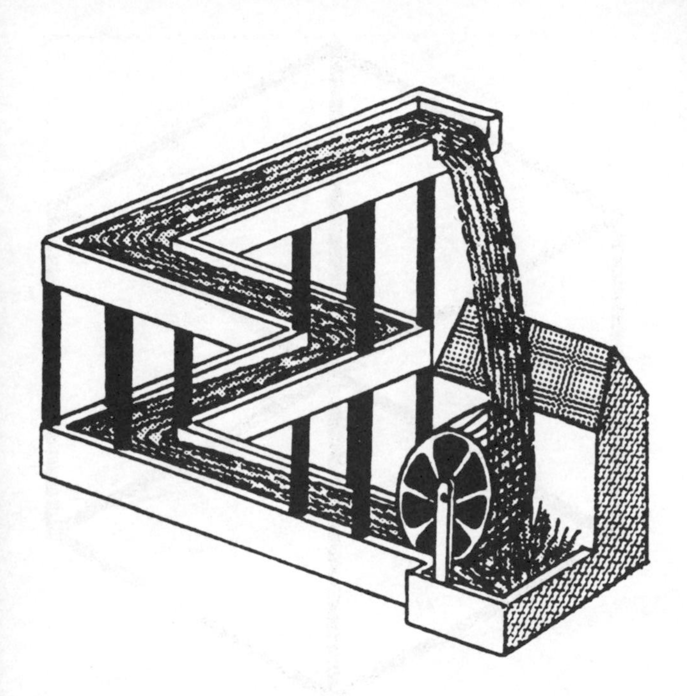

Is this how a waterwheel works?

This hooded monk has a bizarre secret. What is it?

What do you see in this picture?

What is this? Can you decide which is the object and which is the background? A small part of the picture is missing.

Are the stripes in the middle of each circle horizontal? Or do they tilt up and down?

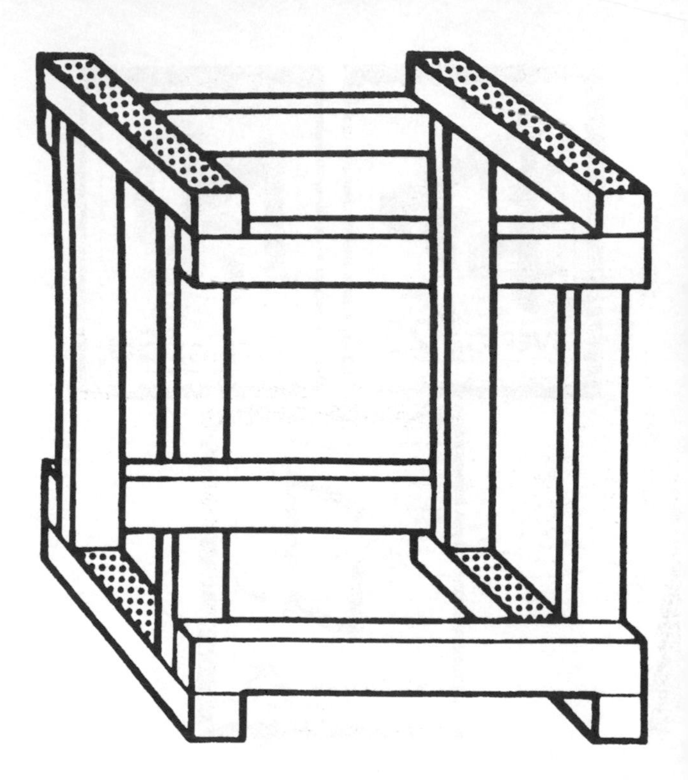

How would you like to store something in this crate?

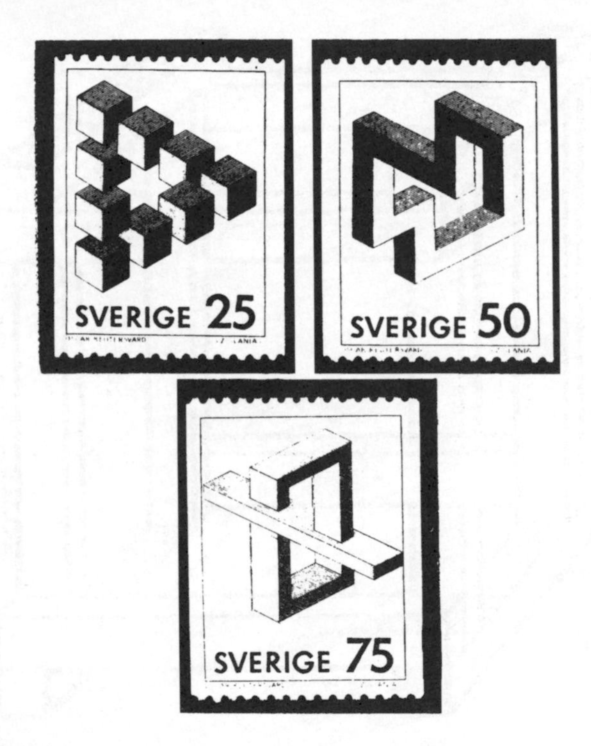

These stamps were issued by Sweden in 1982. They are the creations of Oscar Reuersvard. What do they show?

What is the matter with this picture?

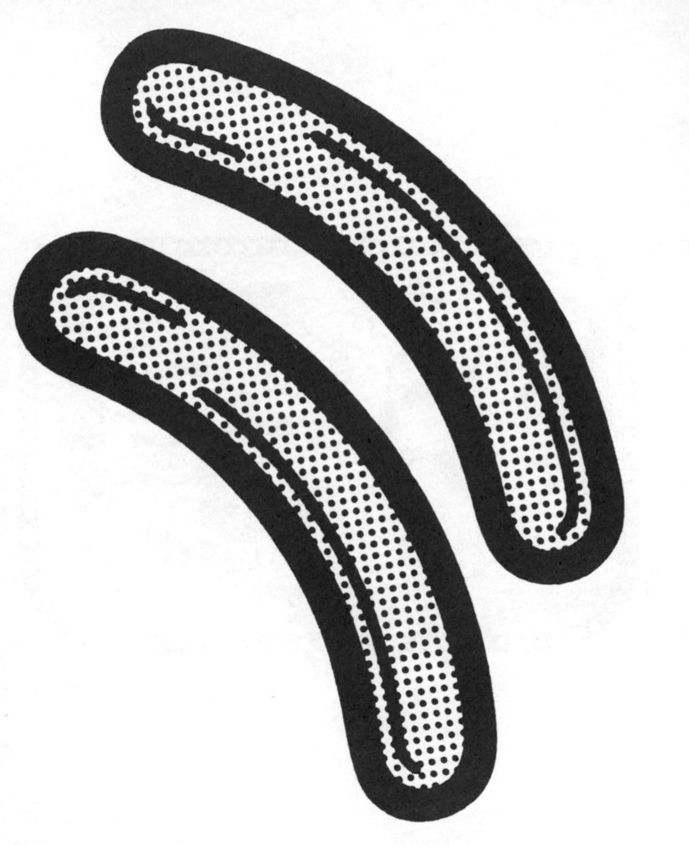

Which frankfurter looks bigger?

This strange woman drank a magic potion and guess what she changed into.

Is this Greek key motif white lines on a black background or black lines on a white background?

The magician is worried that he has lost his rabbit. Can you find it?

Stare at the center of the two gates. Now slowly bring the page toward your face. What happens?

This is the island of St. Helena. Where is Napoleon?

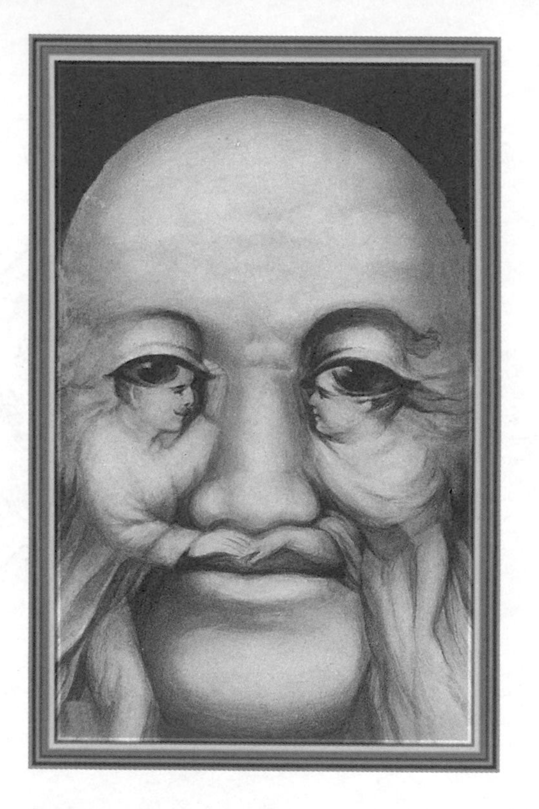

Seen from a distance, this picture looks like a man's head. What else is it?

This picture seems to be bending and
bowing in the center.
Is it really?

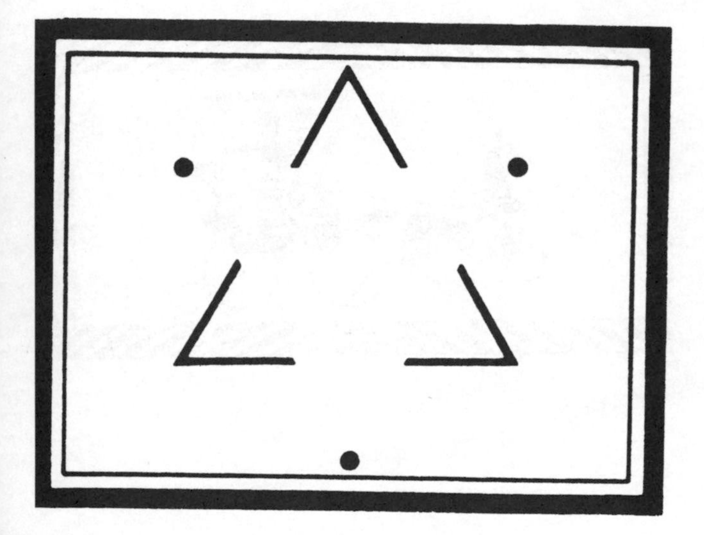

What is unusual about this picture?

a. There is a whole word here. How can you find it?

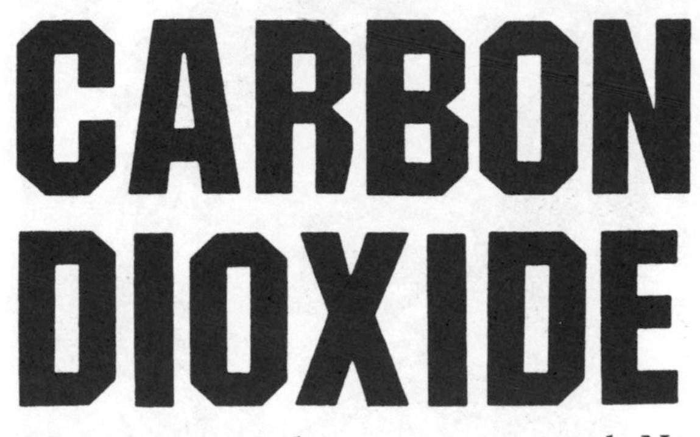

b. These two words are easy to read. Now look at their reflection in a mirror. You won't be able to read them. But–if you turn the page upside down, the word DIOXIDE is perfectly legible. How do you think this works?

This sad milkmaid has lost her boyfriend. Can you find him?

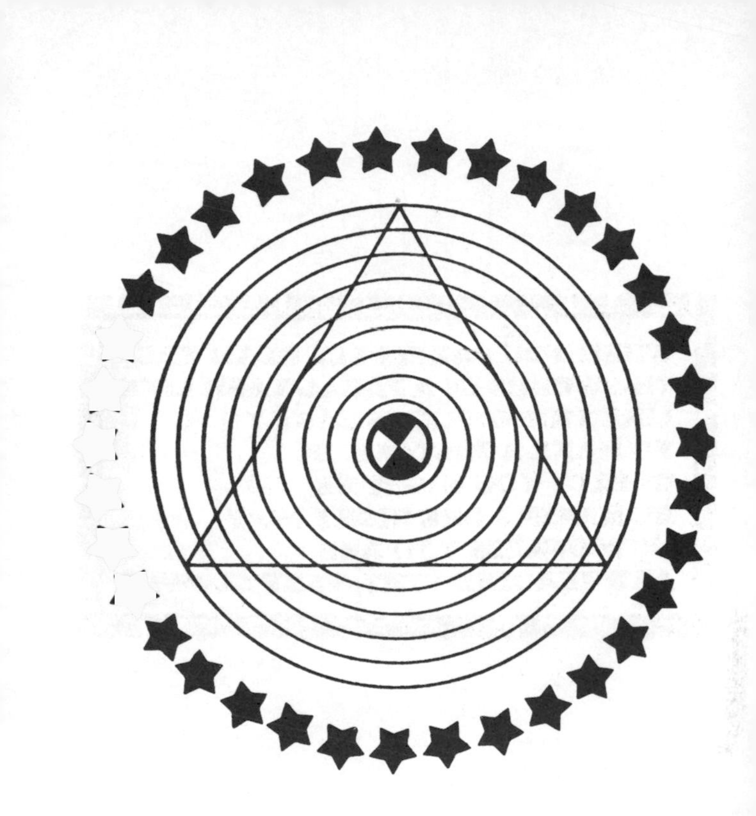

Is this a perfect triangle?

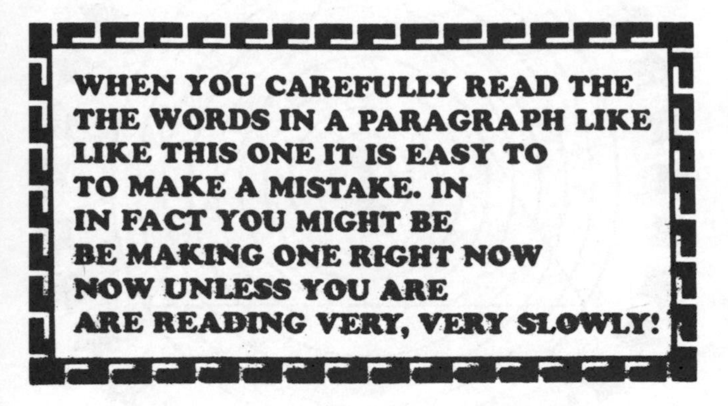

Do you notice anything unusual in this paragraph?

a. Do you see black lines on white or white lines on black?
b. Are the vertical lines parallel?

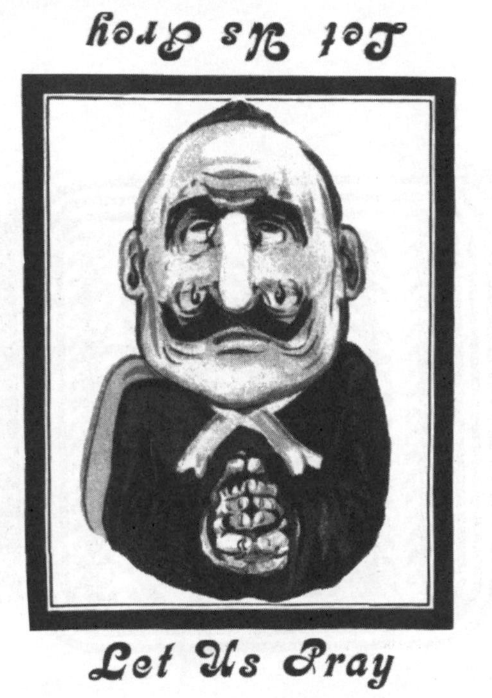

This illustration appeared during the First World War. Why does it have two captions?

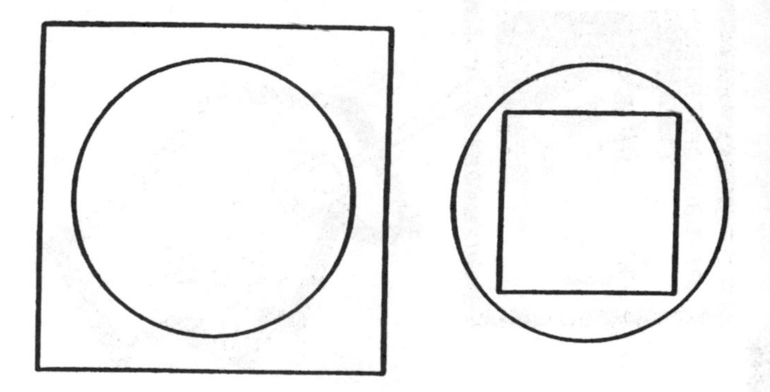

Which circle is bigger?

This stamp was issued by Austria in 1981. What does it show?

Look at the balls the clown is holding. The top one is black with a white cross. The middle one is white with a black cross. What is the bottom one?

This girl is enjoying the Magic Show, but where is the magician?

Which of these flowers has the larger center?

This picture is a bit bizarre. What do you see?

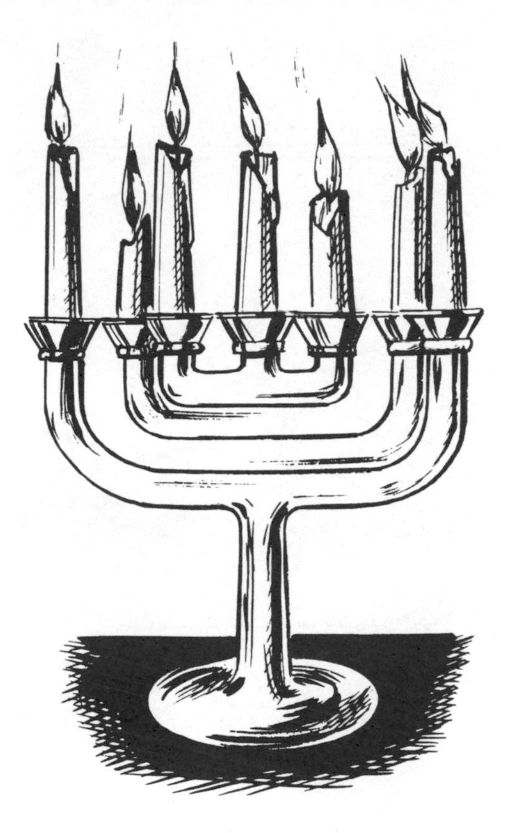

What's wrong with this picture?

Can you find this baby's mother?

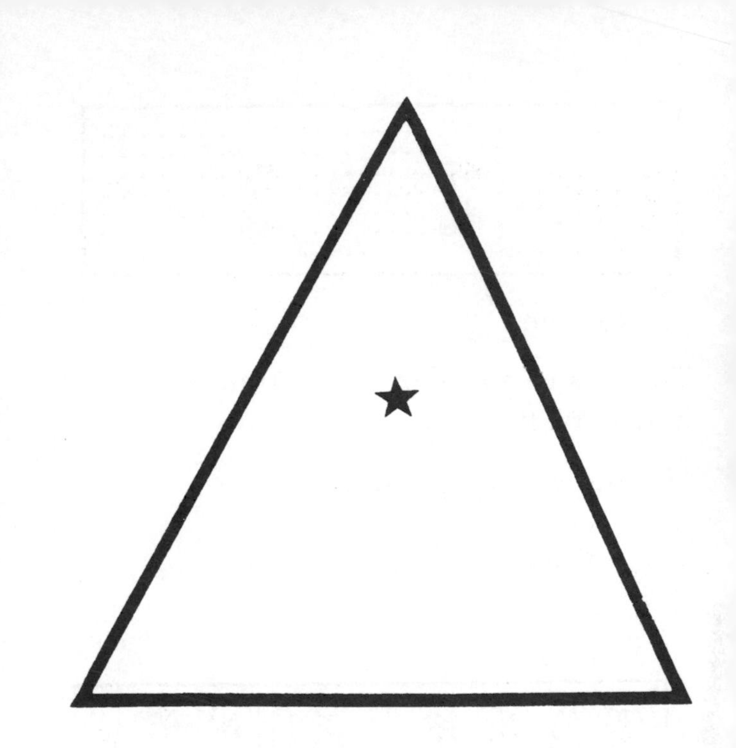

Is the star midway between the point and the base of the triangle? Or is it too high up?

vertical lines.

The dots in #2 seem to be arranged in horizontal lines.

How do you see the dots in #3?

b. The transparent type face used to form the word CONFUSION is called "Bombere." What is unusual about it?

What is wonderful about this early advertisement (besides Puritan Soap)?

a. What's special about these ducks?

b. What is this word? The dots are missing from the I's.

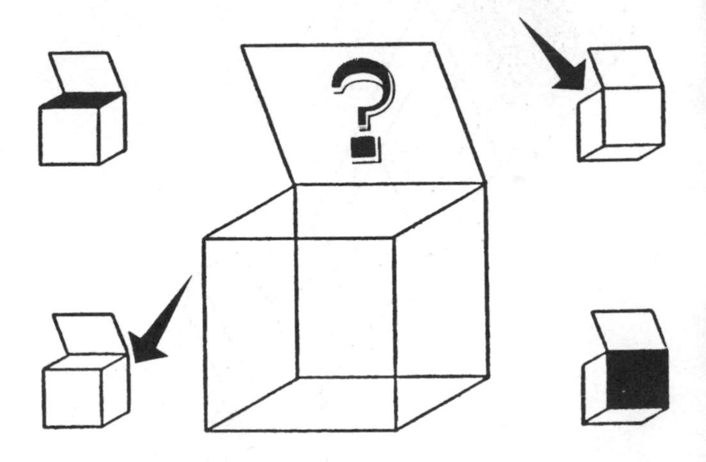

Which way should this box open?

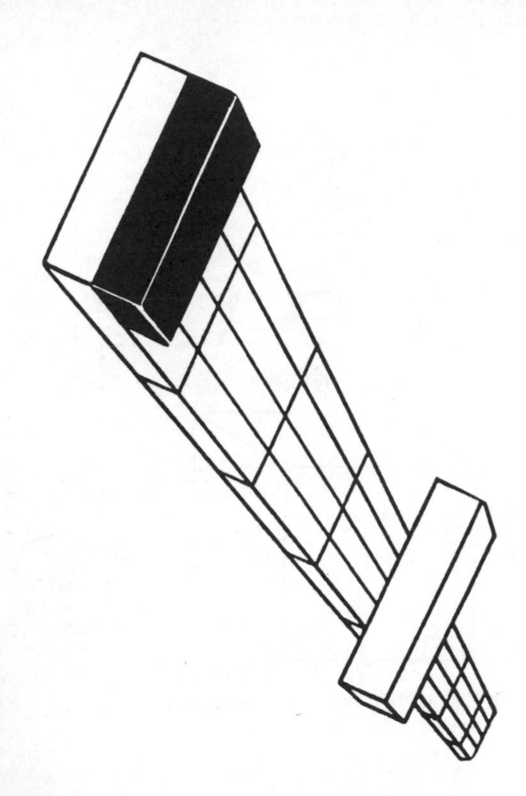

Which block is bigger?

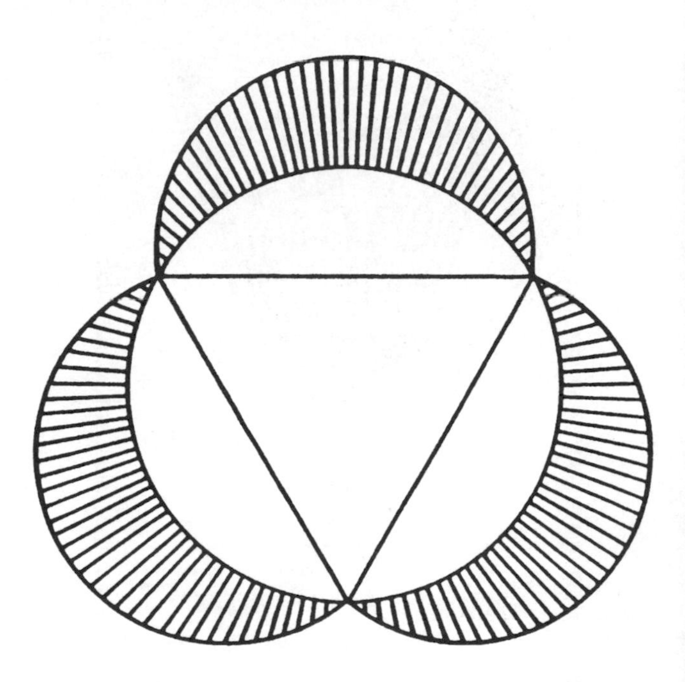

Is the white circle perfect, or is it crimped at the points of the triangle?

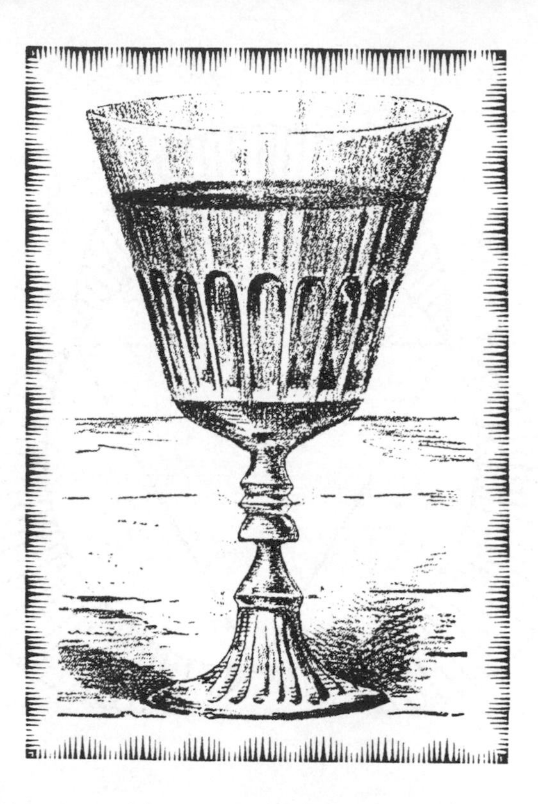

This picture conceals the faces of two men. Can you find them?

Do you think the sides of the cloister arches are disjointed? Or do they join up?

We read this sign as THE CAT, but the middle letters of each word are identical. Yet we see them as H in THE and A in CAT. Why is this?

This stamp was issued in Holland. What is special about it?

What is the matter with the hoop that Geoffrey is holding?

What is this picture?

Is the square sagging at the right?

Which way are the letters facing? Are they pointing down to the right or up to the left?

The patient is worried because his dentist is telling him that a tooth has to be pulled. How can he keep it from hurting?

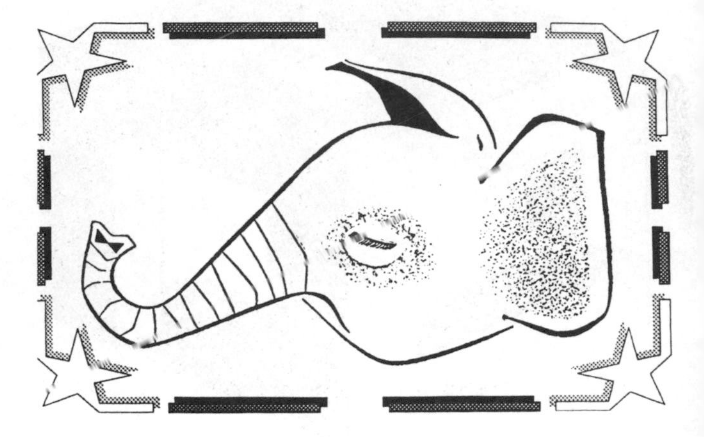

Jumbo the elephant is sad. Can you think of a way to cheer him up?

Can you foresee any problems in trying to make this interesting base for a coffee table?

Can you spot the farmer in this landscape?

What do you think these shapes represent? Look carefully and you may see a three letter word. Once you see it, you won't see anything else.

This mathematical problem is wrong. Can you find the correct answer?

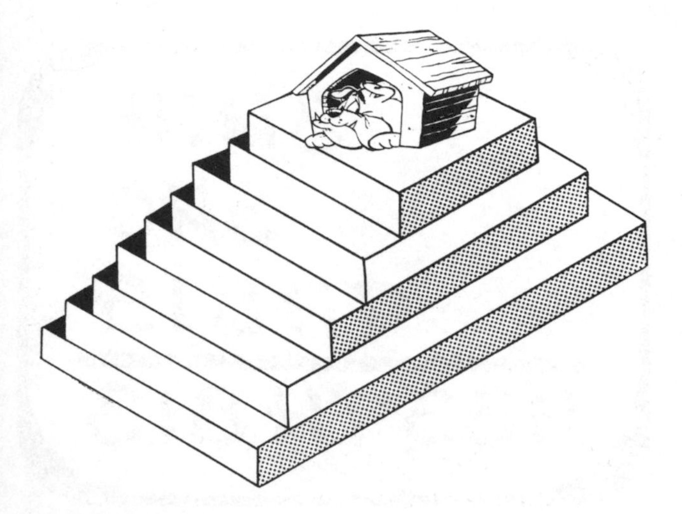

Do you notice anything unusual about this flight of steps?

This fellow helps Santa Claus. But where is Santa hiding?

THE
ANSWERS

Page 6. They are both the same size. Trace one of them and measure it against the other.

Page 7. To find out, turn the page upside down.

Page 8. It says, "I've got a a big head!"

Page 9. It depends on which you saw first–the horizontal A, B, C, or the vertical 12, 13, 14.

Page 10. They are, of course, all the same size, but the perspective lines distort our image of them.

Page 11. The ball appears to spin around!

Page 12. You see a black skull in a white frame.

Page 13. The three donkeys have only three ears between them!

Page 14a. If you measure them, you'll find they're the same size.

Page 14b. Volume 9 (Roman numerals)

Page 15. Look at the picture with the page turned upside down.

Page 16. Theodore Roosevelt.

Page 17. Either one. The design reverses.

Page 18. Look at the left-hand side of the picture.

Page 19. Both. The design "flip-flops."

Page 20. The girl feeds the goose.

Page 21. Guess first, and then use a ruler to line up the lines. Yes, it's "Y".

Page 22. First count the flames–5. Now count the base of each candle, and you'll find there are 7.

Page 23. His mouth looks like a bird and his eyes and nose look like a bat.

Page 24. Turn the page upside down.

Page 25. The set of steps is impossible.

Page 26. See illustration below.

Page 27a. No, it reads "A penny saved is a a penny earned."

Page 27b. ROTATOR is a palindrome. It reads the same backwards and forwards.

Pages 28–29. Benjamin Franklin.

Page 30. Turn the page upside down to find the answer. It says "Life."

Page 31. Take your pick!

Page 32. Both.

Page 33. See illustration below.

Page 34. They are all the same size. The lines of perspective confuse us.

Page 35. You see gray dots that flash and "pop." If you focus your eyes on one of these dots, it will vanish.

Pages 36–37. 1. Top row of meats, first item at left. Some of the lines are missing. 2. Top row of meats, third item from right. The white disk is missing. 3. Bottom row–the last item on the right. The small ring is missing. 4. Bottom row–second item from left. The tail is missing. 5. Bottom row–one of the sausages is missing. 6. Scale. Circle under the dial is filled in. 7. Tip is missing from the pointer on the scales. 8. Meat on the scale has no circle on it. 9. Man's hat is all black. 10. Lines are missing from the inside of the man's ears. 11. Buttons on man's shirt cuff are missing. 12. Two dots are missing from each end on the center band of the barrel. 13. Label on the barrel is filled in. 14. Bands on the legs of the table have been filled in. 15. Trim on left edge of the frame. Some have been filled in.

Page 38. 1691.

Page 39a. 33.

Page 39b. a-b looks shorter, but both distances are identical.

Page 40. Joseph Stalin.

Page 41. Take your pick.

Page 42. They are both the same size.

Page 43. Turn the page upside down and you'll see he has changed himself into a donkey.

Page 44. Actually, the back wheel has been drawn as an oval shape, to give the picture the correct perspective.

Page 45. The shapes begin to look like hexagons.

Page 46. 1. A soldier and his dog walk past a wall. 2. A man gets his bow tie caught in an elevator door. 3. A bird's eye view of a cowboy riding a bicycle.

Page 47. Either one.

Page 48. This is an example of "closure." Your brain fills in the missing bits.

Page 49a. It reads the same when you turn it upside down.

Page 49b. Turn the page upside down. You'd say hello to Uranus!

Page 50. Notice how the underside of one becomes the top side of the other.

Page 51. The curves create the illusion that it's #2, but they are both the same size.

Page 52. It's an impossible figure. Notice how the middle shelf becomes the bottom shelf and vice versa. You can draw this, but you would not be able to make it.

Page 53. At the right distance, the pip on the right side will disappear. And, if you look at the card without closing either eye, and move it toward you, the pips will meet at the center.

Page 54. There are six letter "Fs" in the sentence.

Page 55. The letters in the word all have vertical symmetry.

Page 56. It looks like the lower one, but count the dots or measure the length with a ruler. They are the same.

Page 57. Old Man Mufaroo changes into Little Lady Lovekins in the mouth of a giant bird.

Page 58. Mona Lisa. See illustration below.

Page 59. The line looks as if it's breaking up.

Page 60. It says "Time is is running out."

Page 61. Guess first, then measure. It's #1. Were you surprised?

Page 62. The two cards are the Eight of Clubs and the Queen of Hearts.

Page 63. Nothing, it's perfect–but the sides of it look as if they are bending in. That's because of the background of circles.

Page 64. Either one.

Page 65. Each tube can be seen to open in different directions.

Page 66. To find it, just turn the page upside down.

Page 67. The words in the black panels have horizontal symmetry. That means the letters have the same shape on the top and on the bottom.

Page 68. It is a "magic square." Each horizontal line adds up to 264–and so do the vertical and diagonal lines. It also works if you turn it upside down!

Page 69. Yes, but they look different because of the way they have been placed in the angle.

Page 70. Turn the page upside down to see what he looked like.

Page 71. A small gray disk appears in the center of the spokes.

Page 72. Both sets are the same, but lighter objects look bigger than darker ones.

Page 73. The eyes that have been drawn into the picture of the flag will help you find the faces.

Page 74. Count them at the left side and there are four, count them at the right side and there are only three. It's an impossible picture.

Page 75a. The word "LIFE."

Page 75b. Yes, they are. Hold the page at arm's

length and squint at it. Then try again from a distance of ten feet.

Page 76. It changes direction!

Page 77. The eyes on Grandpa's face have been duplicated. Our eyes find it difficult to understand the repetition they see so they correct for it. At first glance, you probably thought you were looking at a normal face.

Page 78. The horizontal lines are straight and parallel, but the background lines distort our image of them, and they appear to bend and bow.

Page 79. To find out, turn the page upside down. His name is Lionel.

Page 80. Either one.

Page 81. You see flashing white dots bouncing among black dots. When you try to focus your eyes on these white afterimages, they vanish!

Page 82. It's an impossible fork! You couldn't make one, but maybe you can draw it...

Page 83. Between them, these strange fish have only one head.

Page 84. A black cat down a coal mine eating a stick of licorice at midnight.

Page 85. Turn the page upside down to see how the painting got its name.

Page 86. Look at the reflection of this page in a mirror.

Page 87. The bird flies to the perch.

Page 88-89. You'll see two faces on the left and two on the right.

Page 90. They're both the same size, but the arrows make #1 look bigger.

Page 91. Look closely and you'll find profiles of Adam and Eve.

Page 92. It's an impossible elephant. Look at its legs–can you figure them out?

Page 93. Either one.

Page 94. Turn the page so that the arrow points upwards, and you'll see a scene from the circus.

Page 95. Close one eye and bring the other eye close to the page. The checkerboard will straighten out.

Pages 96–97. You can see this any way you want.

Page 98. 6009.

Page 99. "A bird in the the hand."

Page 100. A black rabbit in a white circle.

Page 101. The young woman's chin becomes the nose of the old lady.

Page 102. This is an impossible picture. If the man was really looking into a mirror, he would see his face–not his back.

Page 103. They are the same size, but the arrows make the lower one seem longer. This is called the "Mueller-Lyre illusion."

Page 104. Turn him upside down.

Page 105. The wheels on the bicycle appear to spin and revolve.

Page 106. They are both the same size, but the white one looks larger because darker things seem smaller than light ones.

Page 107. Either one–this is another illusion where the design flip-flops.

Page 108. A beggar holding out a hand–or the profile of a goofy face.

Page 109. They are both the same size, but the curves make #1 look larger.

Page 110. Yes, they are parallel to each other, but the little black squares trick our eyes!

Page 111. No, it's a series of circles within circles. Check it by tracing them with your finger. This illusion is known as the Fraser Spiral.

Page 112. They form an impossible triangle! The idea was first drawn in Sweden in 1934 by Oscar Reutersvard.

Page 113. The print is of two young girls and a dog, but view the page from a distance and watch it transform into a macabre skull.

Page 114. No, they are parallel to each other.

Page 115. Yes, give the page a quarter turn and you'll see his face.

Page 116. Look at the reflection of this page in a mirror.

Page 117. When they open their mouths, a triangle is formed.

Page 118. Turn the page upside down and you'll see why.

Page 119a. Just the way some people start to look like their pet animals, this fellow is getting to look like his musical instrument.

Page 119b. It's the portrait of a man. To see it, hold the book upright and view the picture vertically with only one eye from about 8 inches to the left of the page.

Page 120. It depends on how you look at it.

Page 121. Because this pattern can be viewed from either direction, the brain alternates from one view to the other.

Page 122. Study the picture carefully and you will see his face. His hat is formed from the dog's ear.

Page 123. No. It looks that way because of the way the lines have been drawn, but the square is perfect.

Page 124. Yes, you guessed right–they are both the same size, but most people see "A-A" as the larger distance.

Page 125. Turn the page upside down and see.

Page 126. You might see a medal or 2 men having an argument.

Page 127. Well, it has been drawn correctly at each corner, but the overall perspective is impossible. It looks as though you could make it with wood, but just try it! It cannot be done.

Page 128-129. "Now you see it–now you don't." This is an example of elongated perspective.

Page 130. Yes, but they seem to bulge away from each other. It's the background that confuses us.

Page 131. Two wine glasses–or a wine bottle.

Page 132. Take your pick.

Page 133. Cover their faces so that just their eyes are visible and you will see both sets of eyes are identical!

Page 134. All the bridges are the same size, but because of the way they have been drawn, we believe that the top one is the biggest and the bottom one the smallest.

Page 135. The middle leg is impossible. It disappears.

Page 136. Either one.

Page 137. No, the lines are parallel. It's just the background lines that create the illusion.

Page 138. The one on the right looks bigger, but they are both the same size.

Page 139. Get a ruler and run it along the line to find out.

Page 140. They are the same size, but when one is turned to look like a diamond, it looks bigger!

Page 141. This is called a Jordan Curve–a circle twisted out of shape. Look at it carefully and you will see that the dot on the right is inside the circle, because a line from it crosses the curve an odd number of times.

Page 142. Turn the page 90 degrees counterclockwise.

Page 143. Turn the page upside down and there she is!

Page 144. A broken set of lines? Or a large letter E? This is an example of "closure." Our brain fills in the missing parts.

Page 145. Turn the page upside down and you'll see.

Page 146. Either one. Keep looking at it and it will change.

Page 147. Take your pick.

Page 148. Give the page one half turn in the direction of the arrow.

Page 149. Yes, it is 3 black squares in a white square, and it's also something else–the letter E.

Page 150. No, thcy are perfectly straight and parallel.

Page 151. It's impossible to tell!

Page 152-153. Hold the page in the same way as in the small sketch and you'll see that the pictures are 1. fruit 2. kitten 3. bird 4. house.

Page 154. Bring the page close to your face and the spoon will pop the medicine into his mouth!

Page 155. Simply rotate the page in a circular motion.

Page 156. To read the hidden message, tilt the page–as in the small sketch. It reads, "Can you read this plainly?"

Page 157. Just add 4 lines. See illustration at right.

Page 158. This is actually a perfect square that has been drawn over the diagonal lines. The lines make it look lopsided.

Page 159. It is supposed to be the longest sentence that still reads the same when turned upside down.

Page 160. Joan of Arc.

Page 161. You guessed it, they are both the same size, but the one on the right looks smaller.

Page 162. After you make a guess, use a ruler to check. In this illusion, the outside lines help to convince us that the bottom fish is bigger.

Page 163. To find out, turn the page upside down.

Page 164. Each circle will seem to revolve on its axis. The inner cog wheel will appear to rotate in the opposite direction.

Page 165a. They kiss.

Page 165b. The word "LOVE".

Page 166. Turn the picture upside down to find out.

Page 167. Check them with a ruler, and you'll find that they are perfectly straight rows of tiles.

Page 168. There isn't one there, but we see one that has been formed from the cut-outs of the small black circles.

Page 169. 30.

Page 170. If you saw black as the top of a block you will see 6, but if you saw black as the base of a block there will be 7.

Page 171a. We can read it as "day" or "clay"–it depends on the context.

Page 171b. The lines drawn through the riders and their bikes are what does it.

Page 172. See illustration below.

Page 173. When you turn the page upside down, this nice lady becomes an animal.

Page 174. It all depends on which you read first–the horizontal line or the vertical line of boxes. It can be either "FIR ST" or "FIRST."

Page 175. Take your cues from the small center ring. It can be either way.

Page 176. It is called "the Rubin Vase."

Page 177. Give the page a quarter turn to the left.

Page 178. Noel. (The letter "L" is missing.)

Page 179. The old lady's face shows her life. You

can see her as a baby, a young girl, courting, in marriage, and finally in death. This type of art is based on the work of Arcimboldo, a painter who lived in Italy from 1517 to 1593.

Page 180. Turn the page so that the arrow points downward. It is animal–a dog on a rug.

Page 181. Either.

Page 182. It is either a sitting rabbit or the head of a witch.

Page 183. "TO TIE MULES TO."

Page 184. 56.

Page 185. Eye brow.

Page 186. The man on the right gets stabbed. Touche!

Page 187. Try turning the page upside down. The boat becomes his hat.

Page 188. Yes, they really are! If they were the same width all the way they would look distorted. Check it out on any building with columns. The ancient Greeks were the first to notice this phenomenon.

Page 189. A frog.

Page 190a. They are the same size, but the arrows make us think that the lower lizard is bigger than its friend.

Page 190b. Believe it or not, the little heart is right in the center of the line. If you don't believe it, take a ruler and measure.

Page 191. At a certain point, he will crash into the wall!

Page 192. No, it just looks that way. The vertical and horizontal lines form a perfect square. Its the background lines that make it seem as if they are bulging out.

Page 193. No, it too is a perfect square. The background lines are what make the top look narrower.

Page 194. Turn the page upside down, and there she is!

Page 195. Turn the page upside down, study this man's face, and you may be able to find his wife.

Page 196. This picture has not been finished, but our brain finishes it for us. We are able to visualize the edges of the pages of this stack of books. This is another example of "closure."

Page 197. Turn the page upside down to see.

Page 198. Yes, they are exactly parallel to each other. They look crooked because of the short hatch lines.

Page 199. Nothing. It is a perfect circle. The spokes of the wheel confuse us into thinking it is distorted.

Page 200. The girl's chin forms the grandmother's nose. This is an earlier version of the classic illustration that can be found on page 101.

Page 201a. The wheels seem to spin one way, while the cogs seem to go in the other opposite direction.

Page 201b. The word "the."

Page 202. It depends on whether you're looking at the top side or the underside of the bricks. This is another design that seems to "flip flop."

Page 203. It only looks like a spiral. It's actually a series of concentric circles. To prove that they are circles, you may want to trace one of them with a compass.

Page 204. Turn the picture upside down to see it.

Page 205. Bring the page close to your face.

Page 206. No, it's an impossible construction. You can draw it, but you can't make it.

Page 207. Read the title very slowly. The title is "Once upon a a time."

Page 208. Turn the picture upside down to see the added lines that give Finlay Dunn extra faces.

Page 209. Yes, it's the inner square that makes it look distorted.

Page 210. One way is to use striped wall coverings. They may not be to your taste, but they will make the room look bigger. So will mirrors.

Page 211. Give the page one turn to the left and you'll see the varmint's face.

Page 212. To see Farmer Brown, turn the page upside down.

Page 213. The height of the arch is equal to its width.

Page 214. No. They're both the same size.

Page 215. Try turning the page upside down.

Page 216. It depends on how you look at it.

Page 217. They are both the same size.

Page 218. They share only 3 ears, but it looks as if every rabbit has 2 ears.

Page 219. You will see a black cross in a white square.

Page 220. Turn the page upside down and you'll see why!

Page 221. The spaces around and between letters E Y E. Study them carefully and you may recognize the word "EYE."

Page 222. No, it's a perfect rectangle. The stripes confuse us.

Page 223. Guess first, then measure. The brim is exactly the same as the height of the hat.

Page 224. Turn the page so that the arrow points upwards, and you will see one word repeated across the design.

Page 225. These are impossible pencils, so that while you can draw them, you can't use them!

Page 226. Yes, it is. This is another illusion in which the background lines distort the image.

Page 227. It's a conversation in a foreign restaurant.

Have you any eggs?
Yes, we have eggs.
Have you any ham?
Yes, we have ham.
Okay, we have ham and eggs for two!

Page 228. He will seem to follow you.

Page 229. It is another "Before and After Marriage" illustration, but this couple is different. Turn the picture upside down to see what's going on.

Page 230. No, the lines are the same length.

Page 231. Slowly move the page close to your face. At a certain point, the lines will seem to close up.

Page 232-233. You will see perfectly straight lines and squares.

Page 234. Mouse, camel, snail, clown, goose, human profile, dog's head.

Page 235. Turn the page upside down.

Page 236. A rabbit or a pelican.

Page 237. This portrait is made up of different type faces.

Page 238. See the illustration at the right.

Page 239. "b."

Page 240-241. The woman floats through the magician's hoop.

Page 242. Our brains fill in the missing details, and we see these "shadow" type characters as letters.

Page 243. Tilt the page to eye level and you will see the word "Hello."

Page 244. See the illustration below

Page 245. A grinning face.

Page 246. No, they are perfectly straight and parallel to each other. It's the slanted lines that trick our eyes.

Page 247. Giraffe, lion, camel, elephant, hog, horse, bear, and hound.

Page 248. The clock was upside down.

Page 249. If you turn the page upside down, you'll see that he's a sailor.

Page 250. It says XXV–Roman numerals for 25.

Page 251. Put the edge of a cut-out paper circle over each arc, and find out.

Page 252. Either way. You will be able to see it flip back and forth.

Page 253. It all depends on which set of words you read first–the horizontal line or the vertical line of boxes. It can be read as either USA or LISA.

Page 254. It is made up of many cube shapes, especially in the middle of the design.

Page 255. See the illustration below.

Page 256. No, it is an impossible figure. You couldn't manufacture it.

Page 257. "Love me little" and "Love me long." This style of lettering is known as "Anamorphic Letters" and was a popular way of writing secret messages, codes, etc.

Page 258. Turn the page upside down. It's the symbol of England –British bulldog.

Page 259. To make the ceiling look higher.

Page 260. Upside down, what were peaks appear as troughs and vice versa.

Page 261. It is also a cube.

Page 262. No, it is an impossible figure.

Page 263. Turn him upside down and he looks absolutely the same.

Page 264. Two dancers and two trees–or a weird character with a beard.

Page 265. See the illustration below.

Page 266. They are horizontal. The background diagonal lines confuse us.

Page 267. It's an impossible figure. You won't have a chance to try it...

Page 268. Impossible figures.

Page 269. There are 5 heads, but each body seems to join up to 2 pairs of legs.

Page 270. They are both the same.

Page 271. A goat. To see her transform, turn the page upside down.

Page 272. Either, depending on how you look at it.

Page 273. Of course you can! Turn the page upside down to make the weird rabbit appear!

Page 274. The gates close.

Page 275. Napoleon's silhouette is formed by the outline of the trees.

Page 276. Close up, it's a courting couple.

Page 277. No, it's a perfect rectangle. The stripes are confusing us.

Page 278. There appears to be a white triangle formed from the area within the three small dots. But nothing is actually there. Our mind finishes the picture.

Page 279a. Place a small mirror on the center line. Look into it and you will see a whole word. This works because the letters used all have horizontal symmetry.

Page 279b. The letters are symmetrical in two directions.

Page 280. Try turning the page upside down.

Page 281. Yes. The sides seems to warp, but that's because of the rings.

Page 282. There are several mistakes in it. The last word in every line appears twice!

Page 283a. Both, the design flip flops.

Page 283b. Yes, they are!

Page 284. Because, when you turn it upside down, you see a picture of a very evil-looking character.

Page 285. They are the same size.

Page 286. An impossible crate.

Page 287. Take your choice.

Page 288. Turn the page upside down to find him.

Page 289. It looks like the one on the right, but they are both the same size. What tricks us is the petals around the center.

Page 290. It's a couple, sitting at a table, smoking. Seen from the distance it's a skull. It's interesting that this was drawn many years before people realized the smoking was harmful to your health.

Page 291. Turn on the light–it's the impossible candelabra! A number of the holders seem to be suspended in mid air!

Page 292. If you turn the page upside down and look very carefully, you will see the mother's head. The baby's diaper becomes the mother's bandana.

Page 293. Guess first, then measure. The star is midway between the point and the base.

Page 294a. They can be seen as either vertical or horizontal.

Page 294b. The letters flip flop, so that we can see them pointing up to the right or down to the left.

Page 295. Rotate the page slowly and watch the wheel spin on the woman's finger.

Page 296a. Place a small coin on the head of Duck #1, and the ducks will seem to move to the right. Now place the coin on the head of Duck #2, and the ducks will travel to the left.

Page 296b. "Minimum."

Page 297. You can make this box open in many different ways–depending on which way you want it to open.

Page 298. The blocks are exactly the same size, though the white one looks bigger. This is another illusion in which the background design confuses us.

Page 299. It's perfect.

Page 300. Turn the page upside down. They're bordering the stem of the glass.

Page 301. They join up perfectly.

Page 302. Our brain is trying to make sense of what we see, so it leaps ahead, closes up the top of the second H, and reads it as an A.

Page 303. It is a picture of the Mobius strip, a piece of paper that has been twisted and has strange properties when cut in two.

Page 304. The hoop is actually a circle shape, but here it has been drawn as an oval to give the picture the correct perspective.

Page 305. A mouse–or a man's head.

Page 306. No, it's a perfect square. It looks like it's sagging because of the diagonal lines.

Page 307. Either way. This is another design that flip-flops.

Page 308. Slowly bring the page close to your face, and then slowly take the page away from it. There you are–a painless extraction!

Page 309. Just turn the picture upside down.

Page 310. Yes, it's another impossible object.

Page 311. Turn the page 90 degrees counterclockwise.

Page 312. The word is ELF.

Page 313. Look at the reflection of this page in a mirror.

Page 314. Yes, it's impossible. Count the number of steps. You'll count either 9 or 5 or 3.

Page 315. Turn the page upside down to find him.

ACKNOWLEDGMENTS

The author wishes to thank the following for contributing materials and offering advice: Ali Bongo, Dr. E.A. Dawes, Arthur Day, John Ergatoudis, Ricky Holt, Clifford Hough, Ernie Tongue, T. Stanley Whittaker, Jacqueline Wills, Rose and Pat (Prontaprint) and special thanks to the staff at Bolton Central Library for research help. I would also like to thank Roy Litherland for all his help in proofreading.

I have spent a lot of time and effort and made many inquiries in order to make the data furnished as correct as possible. Unfortunately, in a number of cases I received no reply to my inquiries. The author/publisher would be pleased to hear of any discrepancies so that errors can be rectified. With some of the older material, the originator is not known. Some of it has been reproduced many times without mention of the artist, so it is impossible to give credit where credit is due.

INDEX